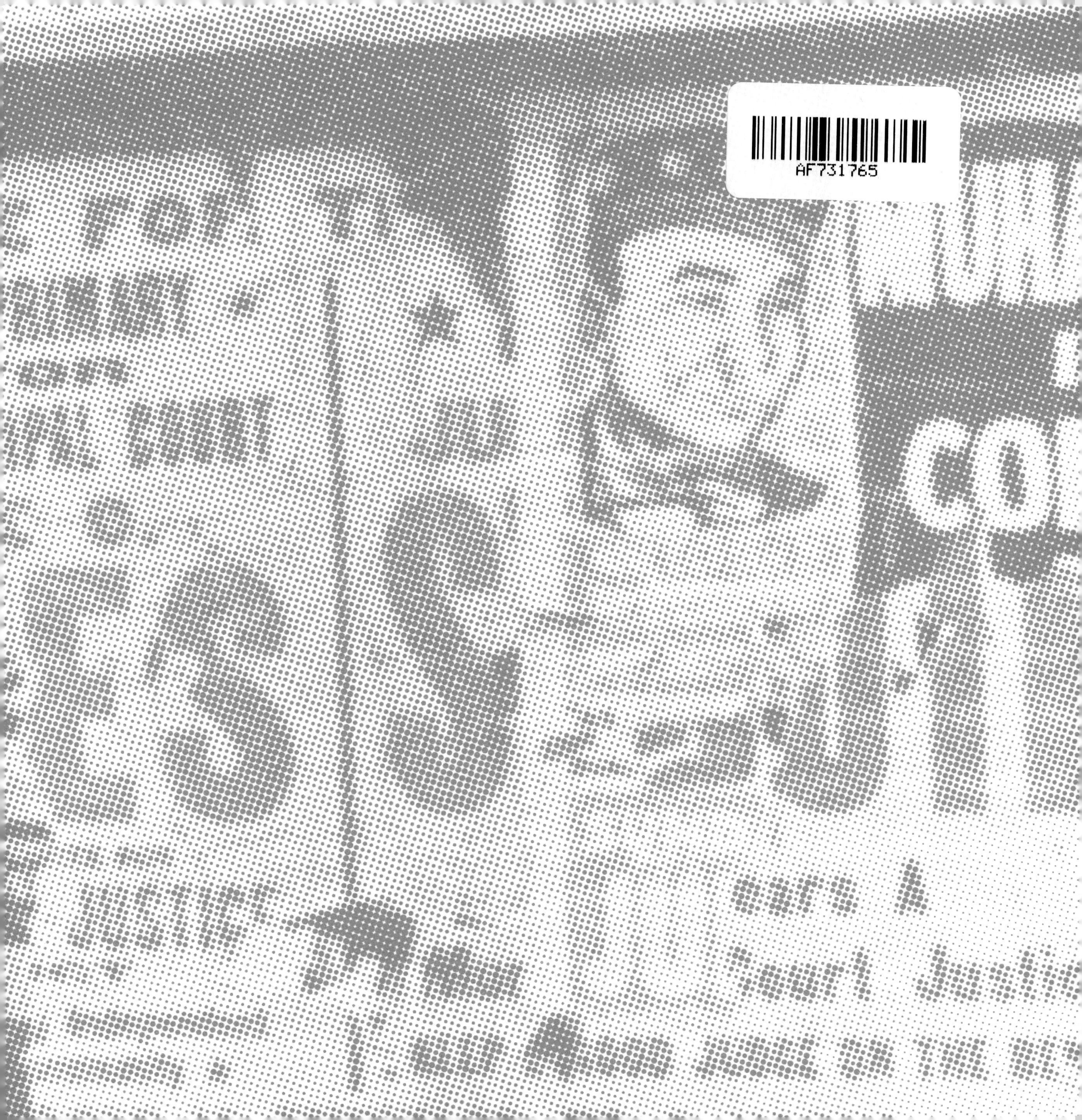

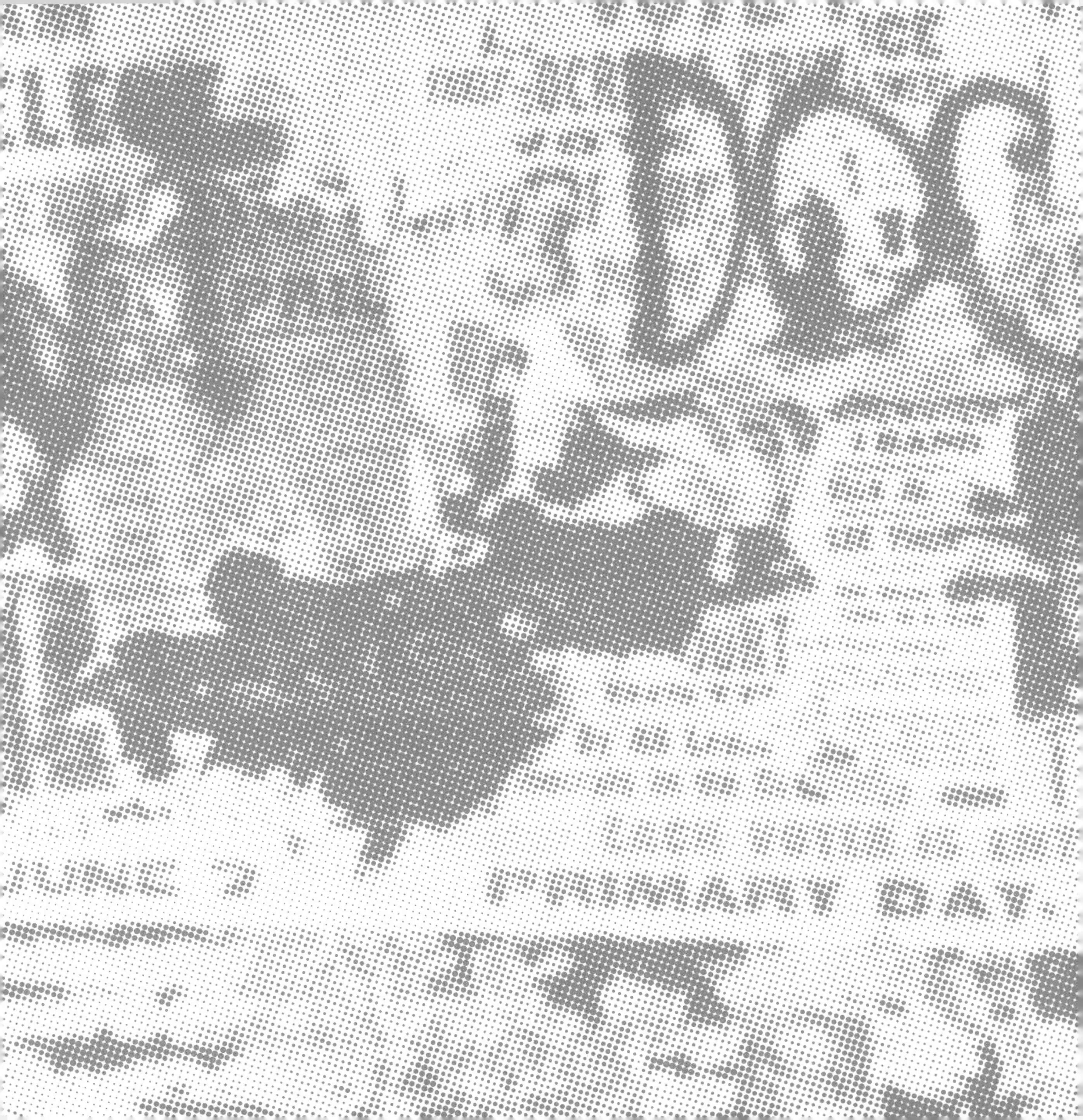
PRIMARY DAY

Unseen

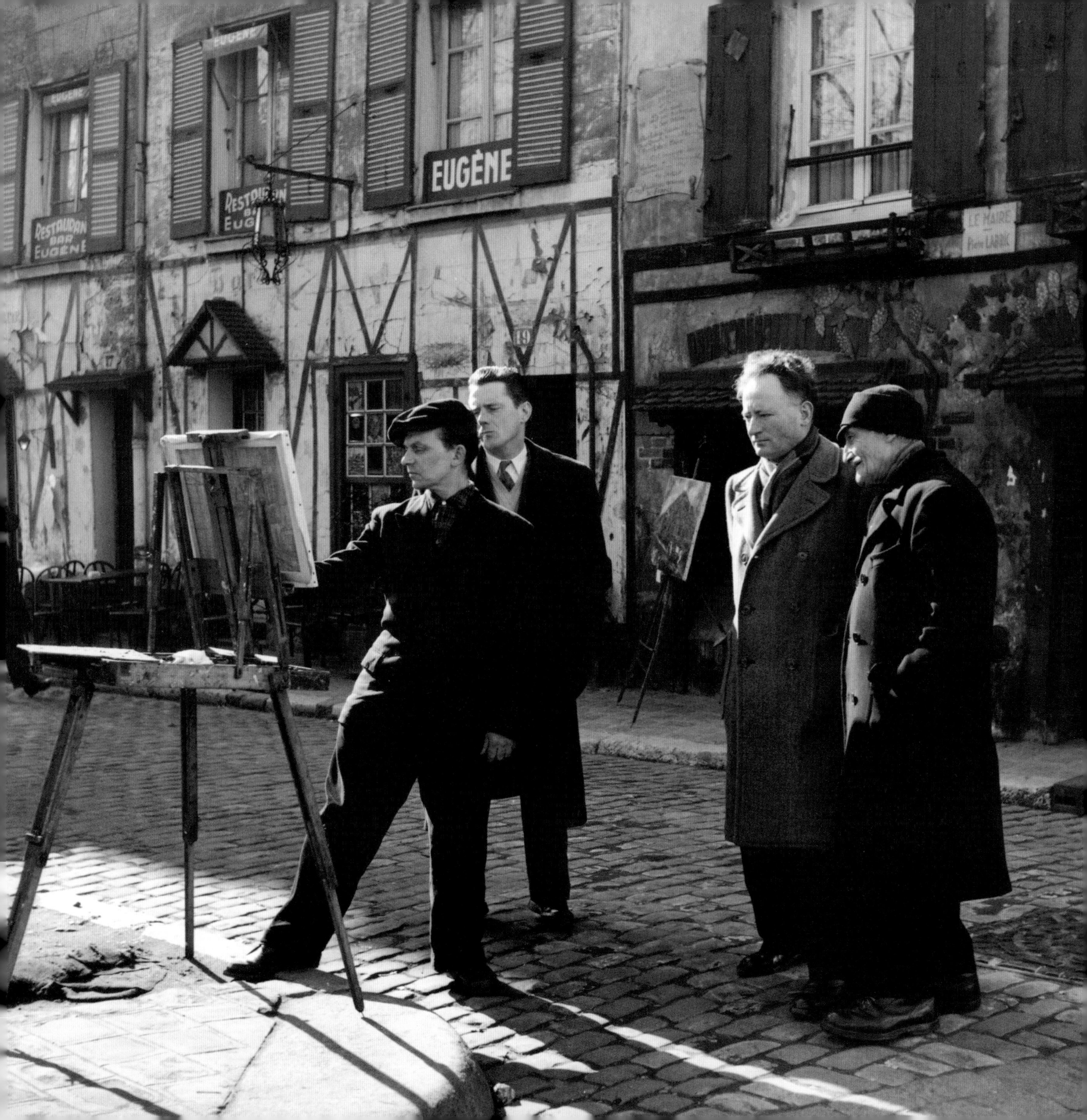
RESTAURAN
BAR
EUGÈNE
EUGÈNE
19
LE MAIRE

Unseen London Paris New York

Edited by Katy Barron

Photographs by
Wolf Suschitzky
Dorothy Bohm
Neil Libbert

Ben Uri | 100
ART IDENTITY MIGRATION

This catalogue was produced to coincide with the exhibition
Unseen: London, Paris, New York
20 May – 27 August 2016

Ben Uri Gallery & Museum
108a Boundary Road, off Abbey Road, London, NW8 0RH
www.benuri.org

A catalogue record for this book is available from the British Library
ISBN 978-1-56581-231-4

Designed by Matt Hervey
Printed by Gomer Press

Contents

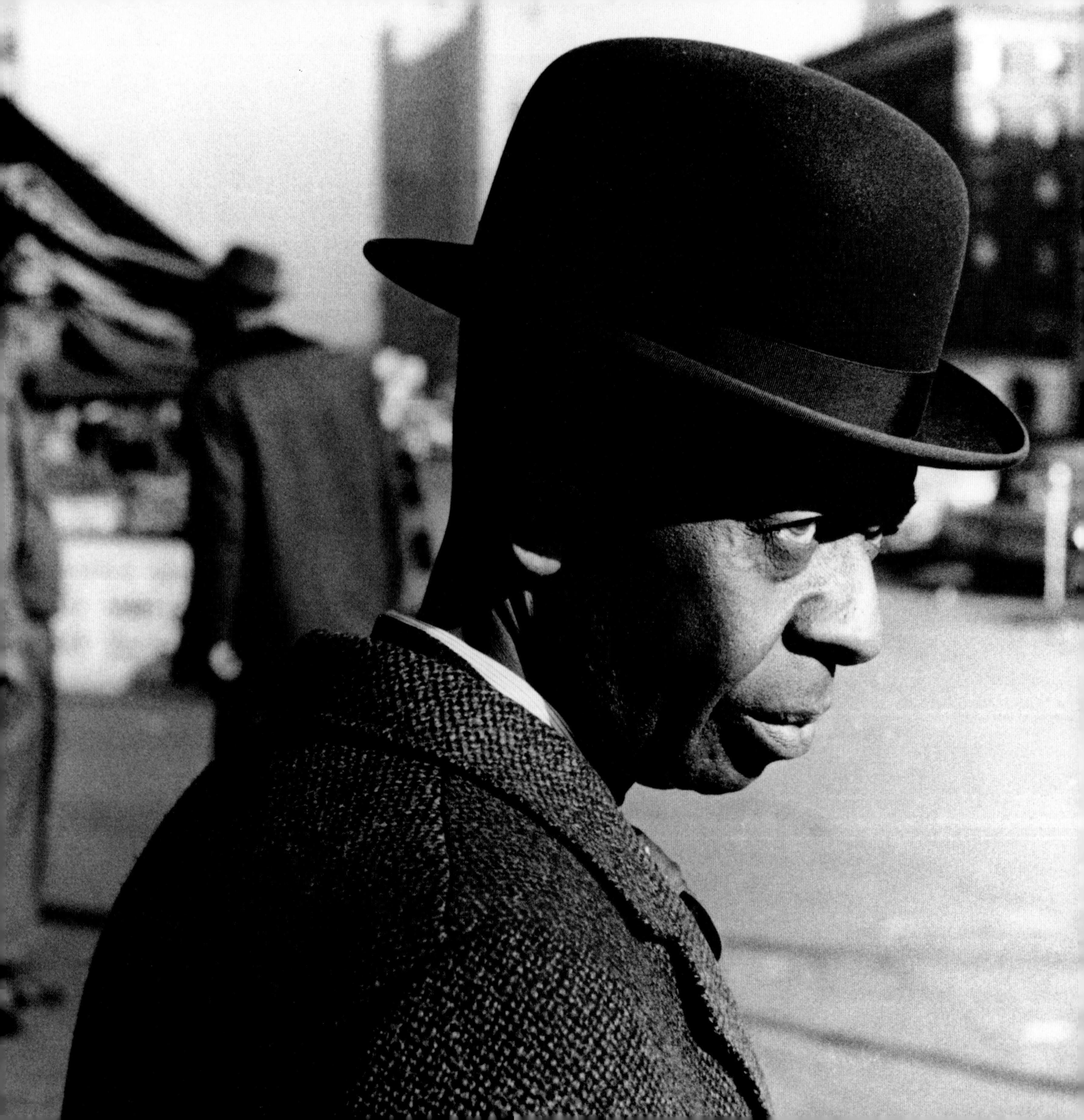

Foreword

Never has photography been more prominent within Ben Uri's 100-year history than in the last decade. The museum celebrates photography as it chronicles the complex personal and artistic journeys of émigré artists, many of whom have redefined the practice and its direction.

Katy Barron, the distinguished photography curator, returns to curate *Unseen* following her successful 2013 exhibition of portraits by Maud Sulter (1960–2008) and Chan-Hyo Bae (b. 1975). *Unseen* continues Ben Uri's focus on the experience of migration, and readers and visitors will encounter 'Unseen' London, Paris and New York through the eyes of Wolf Suschitzky, Dorothy Bohm and Neil Libbert, as they documented their first impressions of the new surroundings in which they found themselves.

The striking combination of metropolitan beauty, social division and political tension that defined the three cities is reflected in a plethora of exceptionally personal studies of their inhabitants. This rarely captured intimacy is a unifying thread throughout the exhibition, while simultaneously evoking a palpable sense of time and place.

Suschitzky, Bohm and Libbert are all part of the rich tradition of photographers of Jewish descent chronicled by Professor Michael Berkowitz in his landmark publication, *Jews and Photography in Britain* (2015). The American influence, from the pioneering work of Alfred Stieglitz (1864–1946) to contemporary photographer Annie Leibovitz (b. 1949), has been more widely appreciated. We hope this exhibition will add to the audience for these three artists and to the European and British heritage that Berkowitz addresses. The fresh and unposed images caught on camera create a vital lens on a time long passed, yet many could have been made yesterday.

We pay tribute to Katy Barron for her scholarship and curatorial skills as one of London's leading experts on contemporary photography. We thank Saskia Rubin who supported her in this endeavor; Matt Hervey for his design for this book; Gomer Press for production; Bayeux Framers for generously sponsoring mounting and framing of the prints; the contributors Michael Berkowitz, Jessica Feather and Zelda Cheatle; the photographers' family members Julia Donat and Monica Bohm-Duchen and her assistant Merita Zhubi; Anthony Hartley of The Photographers' Gallery; the team at Photo London and, most importantly, the artists Wolf Suschitzky, Dorothy Bohm and Neil Libbert for their generous co-operation, support for this project and for their artistry which enriches the lives of all of us who engage.

It is fitting that this exhibition, the finale of the museum's centenary year, presents the work of three remarkable photographers whose vitality today and excitement for tomorrow belie their age – much like Ben Uri.

David J. Glasser, Executive Chairman

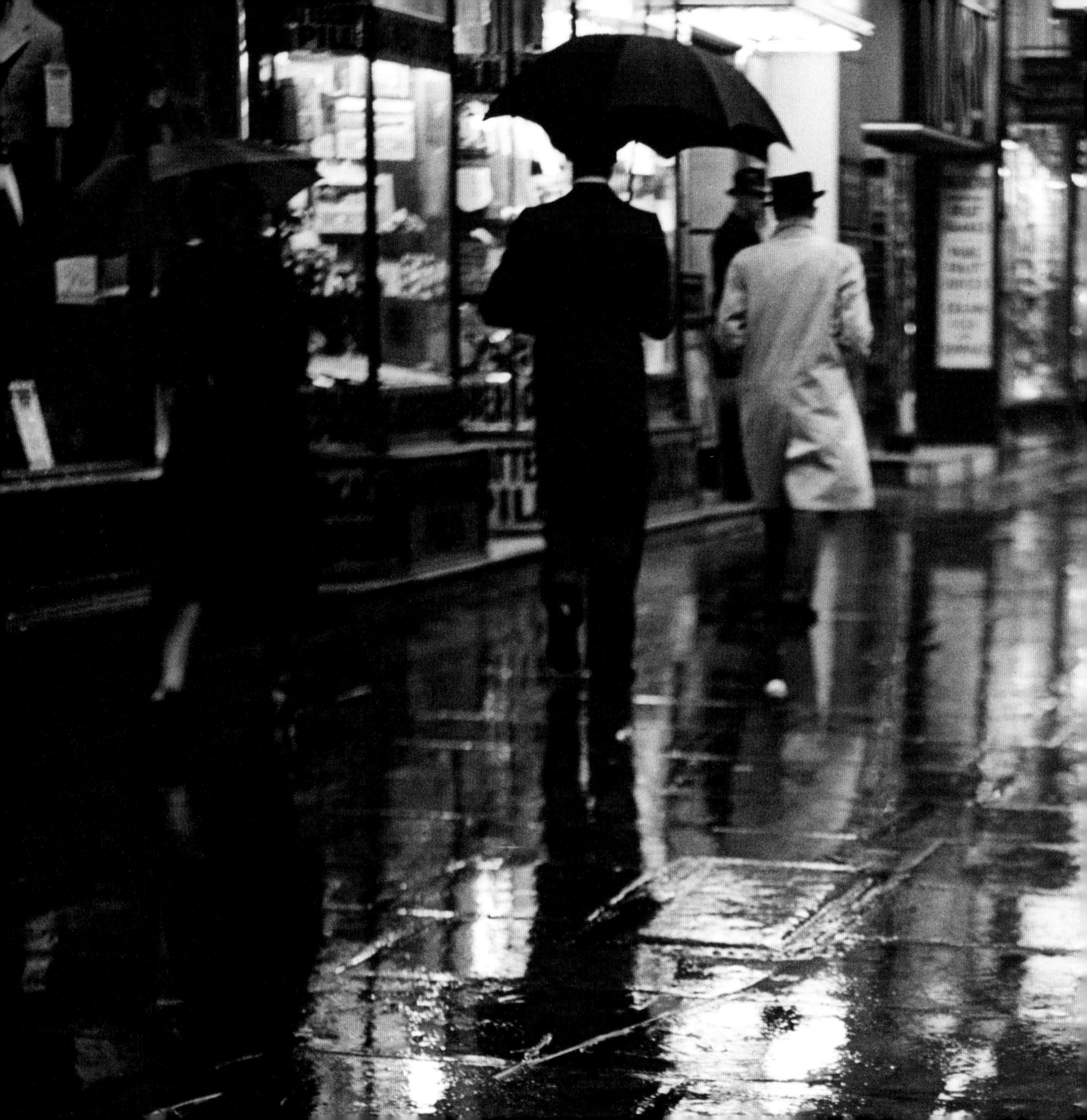

Unseen

Katy Barron

The history of photography has been bound up with city life since its inception in nineteenth-century Paris, and many of our collective visual impressions of great world cities are centred around significant photographic bodies of work, such as Eugène Atget's Paris, Bert Hardy's London or Gary Winogrand's New York. *Unseen* seeks to present each of those metropolitan spaces as encountered and photographed for the first time by an outsider.

This perspective is particularly relevant in the context of Ben Uri, as the museum's origins lie in an art society formed by émigré artists who were outsiders – fleeing Eastern Europe and Russia to seek new beginnings in England from 1915 onwards.[1] In fact, both Wolf Suschitzky (b. 1912) and Dorothy Bohm (b. 1924), who arrived in England in 1934 and 1939 respectively, were part of the second wave of Jewish refugees, fleeing from Nazi persecution after 1933. Ben Uri's important collection includes numerous works made by this generation, such as Frank Auerbach and Josef Herman, and it is well known that these artists injected a raw modernism and realism into the British art scene of the post-war era.

However, Ben Uri, in common with nearly all British art societies and institutions of the time, did not consider photography to be a part of the fine arts, hence photographers were not included amongst its membership and there were no photographs in the museum's collection until relatively recently.[2]

The acceptance of photography as an art form has been a gradual process since its invention and is still ongoing.[3] Equally, the connections between Jews and photography have been long recognised although few have attempted to explain them.[4] As a new reproductive medium that was not quite 'art', the business of photography was well suited to peripatetic Jews on the fringes of respectability during the nineteenth century. Michael Berkowitz, in his new publication, states that 'From the 1850s to the 1950s, if one's picture was snapped for a price, there was a good chance that the person behind the camera was born a Jew'.[5] It is not surprising therefore that two out of the three artists under discussion are émigré photographers, whilst the third, Neil Libbert (b. 1938), is almost certainly from a family of Eastern European immigrants who came to England in the late nineteenth or early twentieth century.[6] Although the connection between Jews and photography is certainly compelling it is important to emphasise that very few Jewish photographers would claim that their faith or ethnicity have played any part in their practice.[7] This is certainly the case with the three photographers considered here, whose Jewishness was a significant factor in their lives' drama but played no role in their career choices.

Wolf Suschitzky first arrived in London in 1934. Unable to obtain a work permit, he soon left for Amsterdam, but returned a year later after his short-lived marriage failed. He went to live with his sister Edith,

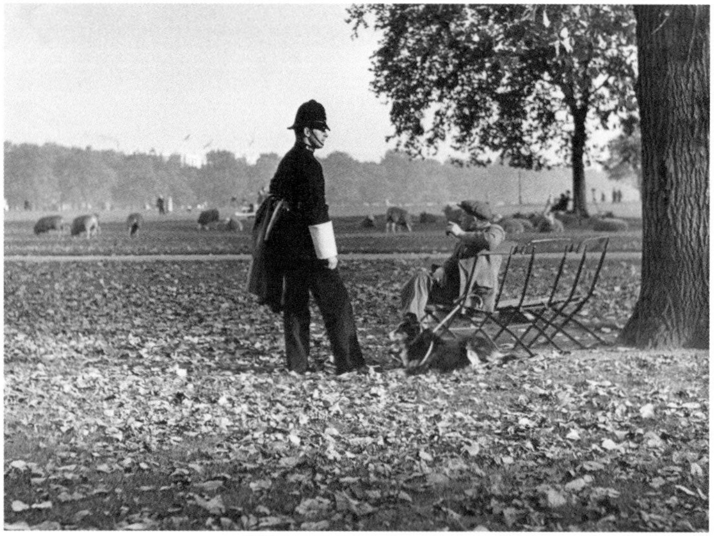

Wolf Suschitzky,
Hyde Park, 1934

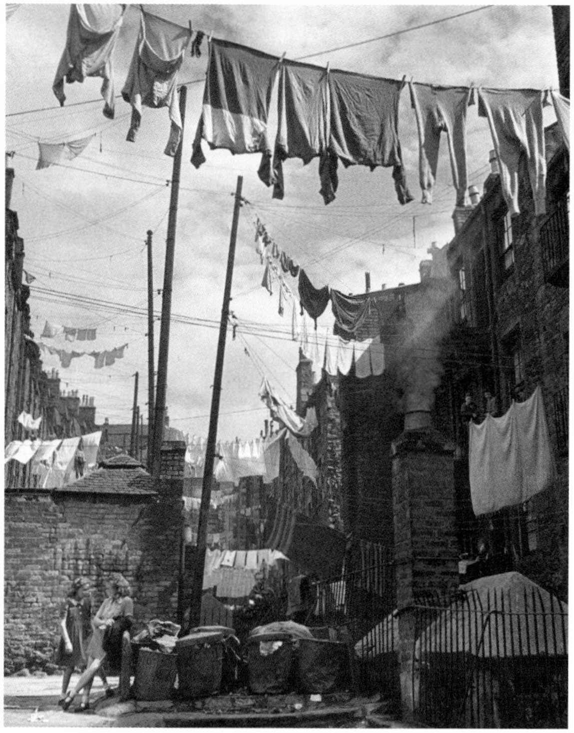

Wolf Suschitzky, *Dundee, Scotland*, 1944

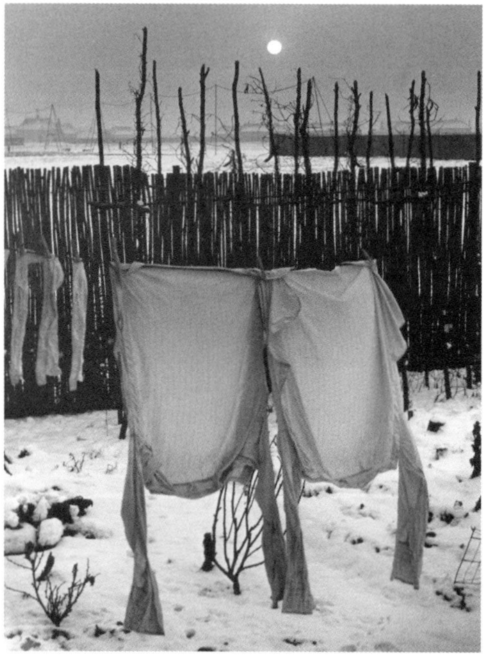

Wolf Suschitzky,
*Frozen shirts,
Welwyn Garden
City*, 1941

now Tudor Hart following her marriage, a well-known Communist sympathiser and successful professional photographer. Their father Wilhelm, who renounced his Judaism and opened the first social-democratic bookshop in Vienna, was an important influence upon both siblings, who were politically conscious throughout their lives. This was to be relevant to both of their photographic careers. Whilst Tudor Hart's practice was driven by her politics, Wolf's approach was quieter – he observed the world and its inequalities but was never governed by an agenda. Suschitzky expressed his artistic philosophy in 1948: 'The photodocument is the reflection of the contemporary scene and represents in its best form, subtle photographic comment on social conditions, rather than direct social propaganda. The human element dominates, and the photographer who has sympathy with social conditions and has been brought into contact with human suffering has in the photodocument a significant instrument for expressing his feelings and usually takes sides'. [8]

Suschitzky and his sister were not alone in seeking both refuge and photographic work in London; 'scores of others would arrive in Britain from the late 1930s to the 40s with press photography as their main vocation; these individuals helped to fundamentally recast the way that the British saw the world'.[9] The photographic scene that Suschitzky and his fellow refugees discovered was ripe for change: 'Our photography was slightly different from the photography people were used to in the UK in the 1930s. Photography here was very pictorial still, romantic, it imitated painting. I did not mind if I photographed a child with a little dribble on its mouth, which they would not have done in a photographic studio.'[10]

The London that Suschitzky found was a place of deep social division, poverty and unemployment as the country struggled to cope with the economic effects of the Wall Street Crash, whilst the National Government disagreed on fiscal policy. This political situation was manifested in the streets through hunger marches and violent clashes, and it was during the 1930s that photography became implicated in the vital political and social questions of the era, as never before. Suschitzky's photographs were not overtly political and they approach these tensions sideways so that the observer is presented with a view of the city that is is so well conceived it is easy to overlook the social conscience behind them. For instance, in *Milkman on the Charing Cross Road*, 1935 the man seen pushing his handcart through the slippery night, (p. 27) could be an extra in one of the films showing at the Cameo cinema behind him, and it is easy to dismiss his back-breaking toil within the drama of the image.

It is well known that Suschitzky was drawn to the bookshops of the Charing Cross Road because they reminded him of his familial and political origins, and that he began to photograph in the area with a view to publishing a photo book. As well as his best-known images of people perusing books (pp. 29 and 45), he photographed a number of tradesmen who frequented the area, such as the street sweeper (p. 31) or the knife grinder (p. 32). Suschitzky's empathy and instinctive respect for humanity is apparent in these street portraits as his subjects appear as individuals rather than 'types' and there are parallels with the particularity of the characters in George Orwell's contemporary documentary *Down and Out in London and Paris*.[11] The strong narrative element to many of Suschitzky's images also points to his later success as a filmmaker.

As an outsider, Suschitzky recalls that he noticed things within the everyday that locals took for granted or ignored – 'Foreigners see things which natives don't'.[12] London's difference to Vienna and Amsterdam – its poverty, smoggy gloom and bad weather – appear frequently in his photographs of the 1930s. For example, the London bus bowling through the snow at Cambridge Circus (p. 41) or the crowd queuing for the cheap seats outside a theatre (p. 44) are scenes that are so particularly 'London', even today, that it is difficult to see them afresh. We can imagine Suschitzky's delight in the bucolic scene of sheep grazing in Hyde Park (p. 38) or relishing the drama of a horse-drawn beer dray charging out of the smoke towards him, like the horsemen of the Apocalypse (p. 39).

One image of Suschitzky's, taken towards the end of the war (the exact date is unclear), deserves analysis within the context of his ethnic Judaism and career as a documentary photographer. He recalls coming across the *War in Wax* (p. 43): 'This is the only obscene photograph that I have ever taken. Walking one day along Oxford Street toward Charing Cross Road, I came upon this shop front. I was too revolted to go in to investigate'.[13] The repellence of the subject matter of the promised dioramas, combined with the mawkish 'Childrens' Section' (see opposite) was recorded in a *Mass Observation* report of 26 January 1944: 'Parts one and two [ie. downstairs and the Childrens' Section] are putrid affairs. There aren't sufficient exhibits to hold (or interest) the visitor's attention. But feeling reaches fever pitch after visiting the "Horrors of the German Concentration Camp" and [the author] is inclined to agree ... that "this part of the exhibition should be open to the public free". It's an excellent piece of propaganda, and conveys far more eloquently, far more graphically, far more forcibly, the Third Reich's interpretation of the "New Order" and provides the perfect answer to the question "what are we fighting for?"'[14] Suschitzky's pin-sharp photograph allows us to read all of the exterior text boards, leaving the viewer to imagine what lies within. His is the only existing photographic record of the *War in Wax* and, as such, it is an important document in relation to questions around the public knowledge of the Holocaust towards the end of the war.[15]

Suschitzky's photographs of London do not reference earlier images of the city – as discussed, the British documentary scene was still in its infancy in the 1930s. The same could not be said of Paris, whose photographic pedigree was incomparable – it was the birthplace of street photography.

Bohm encountered the city for the first time in 1947, having recently begun to photograph outdoors whilst staying in Ascona in Switzerland (see p. 14). Her imagination had been fuelled by French literary and visual culture for many years and it is easy to imagine her arrival in Paris, after the ordeals of wartime Manchester, as an epiphany.

Bohm has photographed Paris throughout her life and it is fitting that her images of the city were the subject of a solo exhibition, *Un amour de Paris*, at the Musée Carnavalet in 2005.[16] Her earliest black and white works (she turned to colour in the 1980s), were taken between her first visit and 1955, when she left the city after a year's residence, as her husband was offered a job in the United States. These works, a selection of which are presented here, are evidence of Bohm's newly found artistic and physical freedom as she made images outside the environs of the studio, away from the intellectual and visual boundaries associated with the portrait-maker's trade. Bohm was not part of the flourishing photography scene that developed in post-war France but rather kept to herself, seeking encouragement from the artist Avigdor Arikha (1929–2010) who had arrived in the city in 1948. Whilst she acknowledges

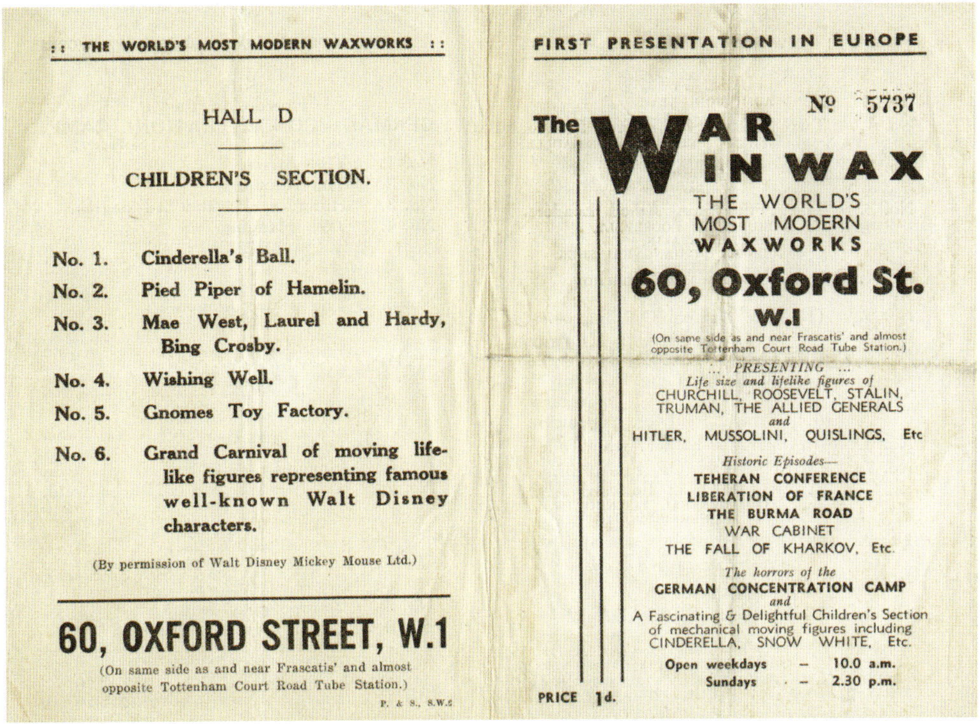

:: THE WORLD'S MOST MODERN WAXWORKS ::

HALL D

CHILDREN'S SECTION.

No. 1. Cinderella's Ball.

No. 2. Pied Piper of Hamelin.

No. 3. Mae West, Laurel and Hardy, Bing Crosby.

No. 4. Wishing Well.

No. 5. Gnomes Toy Factory.

No. 6. Grand Carnival of moving life-like figures representing famous well-known Walt Disney characters.

(By permission of Walt Disney Mickey Mouse Ltd.)

60, OXFORD STREET, W.1

(On same side as and near Frascatis' and almost opposite Tottenham Court Road Tube Station.)

P. & S., S.W.2

FIRST PRESENTATION IN EUROPE

№ 5737

The WAR IN WAX

THE WORLD'S MOST MODERN WAXWORKS

60, Oxford St. W.1

(On same side as and near Frascatis' and almost opposite Tottenham Court Road Tube Station.)

... *PRESENTING* ...

Life size and lifelike figures of

CHURCHILL, ROOSEVELT, STALIN, TRUMAN, THE ALLIED GENERALS

and

HITLER, MUSSOLINI, QUISLINGS, Etc

Historic Episodes—

TEHERAN CONFERENCE

LIBERATION OF FRANCE

THE BURMA ROAD

WAR CABINET

THE FALL OF KHARKOV, Etc.

The horrors of the

GERMAN CONCENTRATION CAMP

and

A Fascinating & Delightful Children's Section of mechanical moving figures including CINDERELLA, SNOW WHITE, Etc.

Open weekdays – 10.0 a.m.

Sundays – 2.30 p.m.

PRICE 1d.

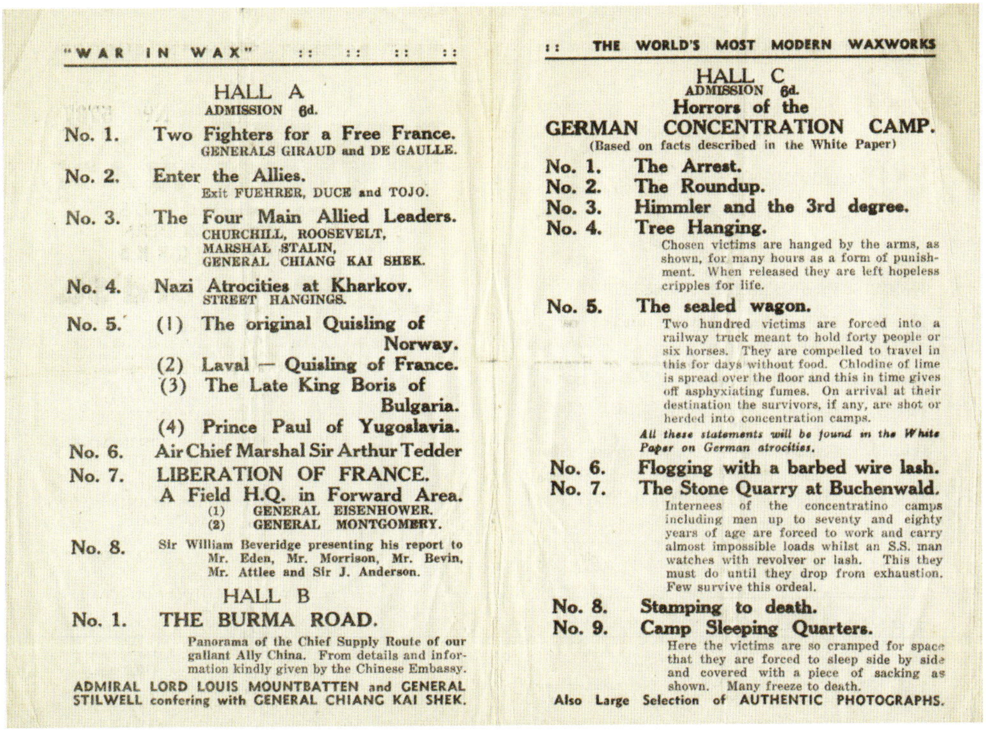

"WAR IN WAX" :: :: :: ::

HALL A

ADMISSION 6d.

No. 1. Two Fighters for a Free France. GENERALS GIRAUD and DE GAULLE.

No. 2. Enter the Allies. Exit FUEHRER, DUCE and TOJO.

No. 3. The Four Main Allied Leaders. CHURCHILL, ROOSEVELT, MARSHAL STALIN, GENERAL CHIANG KAI SHEK.

No. 4. Nazi Atrocities at Kharkov. STREET HANGINGS.

No. 5. (1) The original Quisling of Norway.

(2) Laval — Quisling of France.

(3) The Late King Boris of Bulgaria.

(4) Prince Paul of Yugoslavia.

No. 6. Air Chief Marshal Sir Arthur Tedder

No. 7. LIBERATION OF FRANCE.

A Field H.Q. in Forward Area.

(1) GENERAL EISENHOWER.

(2) GENERAL MONTGOMERY.

No. 8. Sir William Beveridge presenting his report to Mr. Eden, Mr. Morrison, Mr. Bevin, Mr. Attlee and Sir J. Anderson.

HALL B

No. 1. THE BURMA ROAD.

Panorama of the Chief Supply Route of our gallant Ally China. From details and information kindly given by the Chinese Embassy.

ADMIRAL LORD LOUIS MOUNTBATTEN and GENERAL STILWELL confering with GENERAL CHIANG KAI SHEK.

:: THE WORLD'S MOST MODERN WAXWORKS

HALL C

ADMISSION 6d.

Horrors of the GERMAN CONCENTRATION CAMP.

(Based on facts described in the White Paper)

No. 1. The Arrest.

No. 2. The Roundup.

No. 3. Himmler and the 3rd degree.

No. 4. Tree Hanging.

Chosen victims are hanged by the arms, as shown, for many hours as a form of punishment. When released they are left hopeless cripples for life.

No. 5. The sealed wagon.

Two hundred victims are forced into a railway truck meant to hold forty people or six horses. They are compelled to travel in this for days without food. Chlodine of lime is spread over the floor and this in time gives off asphyxiating fumes. On arrival at their destination the survivors, if any, are shot or herded into concentration camps.

All these statements will be found in the White Paper on German atrocities.

No. 6. Flogging with a barbed wire lash.

No. 7. The Stone Quarry at Buchenwald.

Internees of the concentratino camps including men up to seventy and eighty years of age are forced to work and carry almost impossible loads whilst an S.S. man watches with revolver or lash. This they must do until they drop from exhaustion. Few survive this ordeal.

No. 8. Stamping to death.

No. 9. Camp Sleeping Quarters.

Here the victims are so cramped for space that they are forced to sleep side by side and covered with a piece of sacking as shown. Many freeze to death.

Also Large Selection of AUTHENTIC PHOTOGRAPHS.

The War in Wax visitor guide, c. 1944–45

Dorothy Bohm, *Ascona*, late 1940s

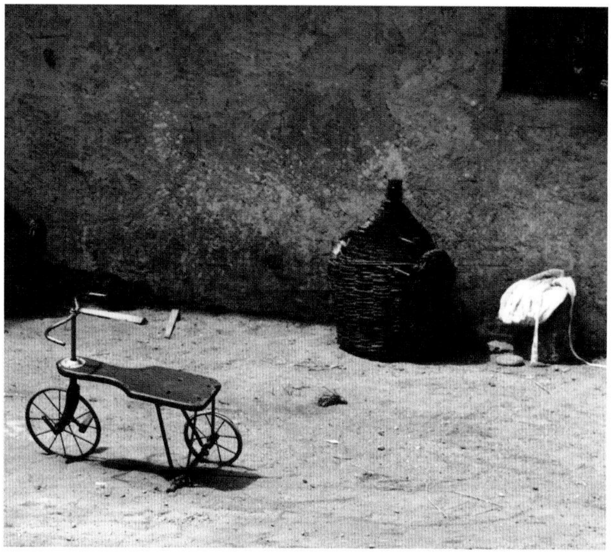

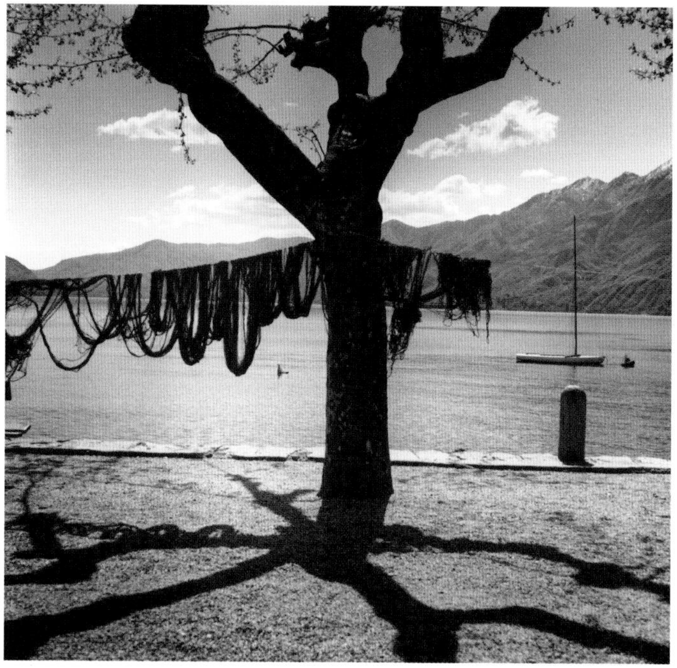

Dorothy Bohm, *Lago Maggiore, Ticino*, 1950

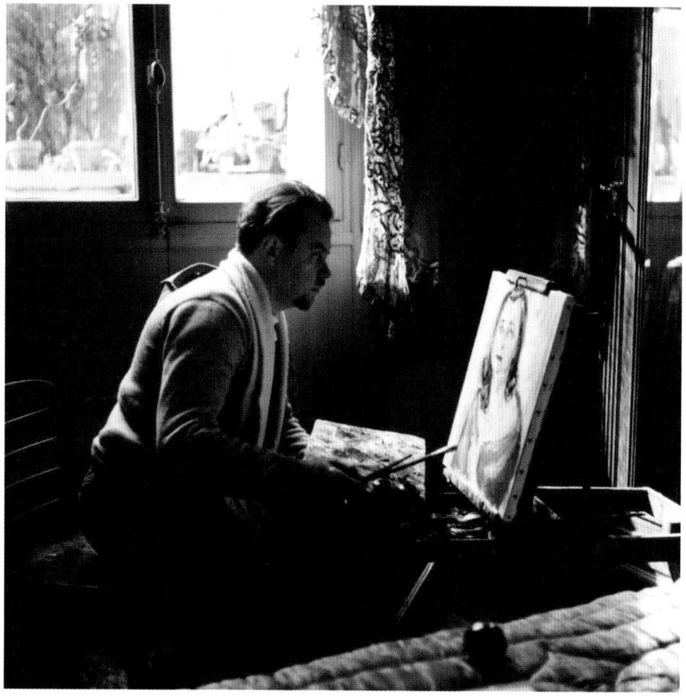

Dorothy Bohm, *Artist with Portrait of Dorothy on Easel, Montmartre*, 1954

that there are similarities between her work and those of the Humanists, such as Willy Ronis or Robert Doisneau, these are purely accidental as the latter made work for mass publication which sought to convey a quintessential Frenchness to an eager post-war readership. Bohm's exploration of post-war Paris was driven by an energetic quest to see and to understand the city through the camera lens and the resulting images were not exhibited until much later.

Miraculously, Paris was almost unscathed by the war, and the violent social dramas of the post-war years were played out against a physical backdrop that was essentially unchanged for centuries. However, the wear and tear of the inter-war years and the Occupation had left a city that was painfully neglected and in the grip of austerity. Bohm recorded both of these faces of the city in unpeopled images that focus on the interplay of structural form and light. In *The Seine, Quai du Louvre and Pont-Neuf,* 1955 (p. 68), which could be paying homage to Atget, she captures the abstracted beauty of the architectural backbones of the city. Equally, her lens focuses on forms of dilapidation and ruin in *Near the Old Les Halles Market*, 1953 (p. 58). Both images use light and perspective with such subtlety that the viewer could be forgiven for overlooking the complexity of both compositions.

Bohm's extraordinary freedom in Paris – she was under no economic pressure and had no political agenda – is expressed in the range of her subject matter, although she often returns to the theme of patient spectatorship, either watching others at work (pp. 56 and 61), waiting for customers (p. 57) or strangers observing Bohm herself (p. 67). Bohm presents Paris as the stage for a series of quiet, almost melancholy, narratives that remind us of her admiration for her long-term friend André Kertész (1894–1985). There are no young lovers kissing, noble workers toiling or dramatic vistas in her compositions and this sets her apart from her Humanist contemporaries.[17]

Bohm suggests that as a woman she was more able to photograph strangers close up and it might be that this, coupled with her youth, which enabled her to photograph children so well. A comparison could be made between the young siblings that Bohm photographed in *Rue Tholozé, Montmartre*, in 1954 (p. 60) *Rue Mouffetard* by Henri Cartier-Bresson (1908–2004), taken the same year. The parallels between the images are remarkable. What sets Bohm's photograph apart is the stillness of her image and the siblings' awkward uncertainty as the older brother takes responsibility for his sister after crossing the road together. Whilst Cartier-Bresson's carefree cheeky subject was photographed on the move, at an angle from above, Bohm's portrait feels more composed, perhaps as a result of her years in the studio. Her composition is not about the 'decisive moment' – the catchphrase synonymous with the work of Cartier-Bresson. Rather, she seeks to convey a truth about two particular children at that time and place and their familial relationships as well their, albeit brief, relationship to the camera.

Whilst Suschitzky and Bohm's photographs document the adversity they found in London and Paris respectively (pp. 37 and 54), Neil Libbert's earlier New York images convey the optimism and energy of a city that considered itself the economic, political and cultural capital of the world (p. 87). Such confidence was short-lived, and as the decade continued, it became the crucible for industrial and civil unrest as well as increasing economic and social decay, leading to the fiscal crisis of the early 1970s when the city neared bankruptcy. Libbert's photographs in this exhibition reflect all of these contradictory aspects of New York. His first visit, in 1960, was in the company of William J. Weatherby, a fellow staff writer from the *Manchester Guardian*. Weatherby was later to settle in the United States, producing numerous publications including a biography of his friend James Baldwin (New York, 1989) and *The Negro in New York: An informal Social History, 1626–1940* (New York, 1967). The latter was published by Frederick A. Praeger, a Jewish refugee who had, like Wilhelm Suschitzky, worked in publishing in Vienna.[18] Praeger published a number of titles that gave American readers their first incisive views of life under Communism, including the first English translations of works by Aleksandr Solzhenitsyn and Milovan Djilas. It is possible that Libbert and Praeger may have met through Weatherby. Indeed, Libbert recalls how he stayed at the Chelsea Hotel during his early visits to New York and it is tempting to imagine him moving within the famously radical creative circles of the era.

Libbert arrived in New York at a seminal moment in the history of documentary photography. Gary Winogrand, Diane Arbus and Lee Friedlander, all second generation Jews, were working in the city, reinventing the documentary tradition and altering the practice of photography irrevocably. Their work was the subject of John Szarkowski's landmark exhibition, *New Documents*, at MoMA in 1967. He writes, 'In the past decade a new generation of photographers has redirected the technique and aesthetic of documentary photography to more personal ends. Their aim has been not to reform life but to know it, not to persuade but to understand. The world, in spite of its terrors, is approached as the ultimate source of wonder and fascination, no less precious for being irrational and incoherent.'[19] Some of Libbert's photographs, such as *Lower East Side*, 1964 (p. 94) reflect these new approaches as well as those of the New York Photo League, a group composed mainly of Jews, who photographed across the city between 1936 and 1951 with the intention of bringing the plight of its inhabitants to public attention through idealistic documentary work.

Many of Libbert's New York photographs appear to have been taken discreetly, reflecting both his natural reserve and huge charm, traits that might explain how he was able to photograph in Harlem so frequently (pp. 78, 79, 84, 95, 99). His most arresting Harlem photograph, *Harlem Race Riots*, 1964 (pp. 84) is a barely concealed commentary on race and politics, as a small boy confronts a seemingly huge policeman with a replica gun in a scene that evokes David and Goliath. The skewed composition, the policeman's cut-off head and legs and the huge empty space between the protagonists combine to create a powerful image that lies somewhere between reportage and the work of the new documentary photographers. In fact, Libbert was to photograph riots again, this time in Brixton, London, in 1981 and he recalled how frightening the Harlem riots were in a newspaper interview about his Brixton images.[20] Apart from Harlem, Libbert's New York subject matter ranges hugely, from timeless skaters (p. 93) to a subtle commentary on consumerism (p. 90) and it is perhaps this democratic view that marks him as an outsider. He plays with concealed light sources to great effect in *Grand Central Station*, 1960 (p. 80) and *Wall Street*, 1960 (p. 81), whilst both *Nightlife, Broadway*, 1960 (p. 86) and *42nd Street*, 1960 (p. 88) distort the subject through the angle of the composition and focus. The two latter pictures tell parallel stories – two women, one young and one old, are both about to enter or exit cars that are parked up by men who mirror their age. We see just enough of the younger woman to imagine

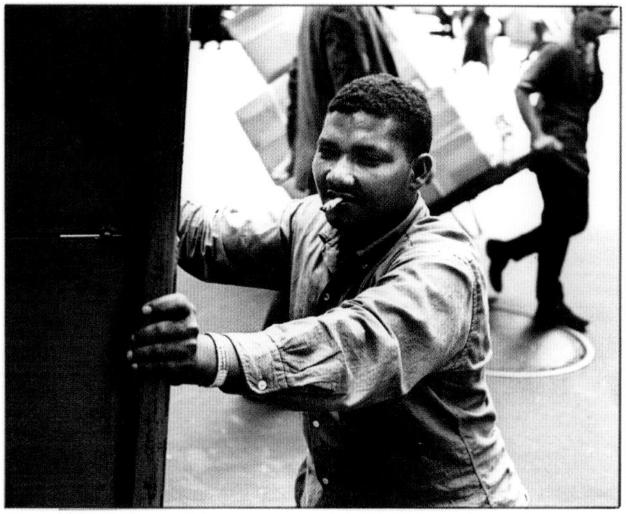

Neil Libbert, *7th Ave, Garment District*, 1966

Neil Libbert, *Guggemheim Museum*, 1960

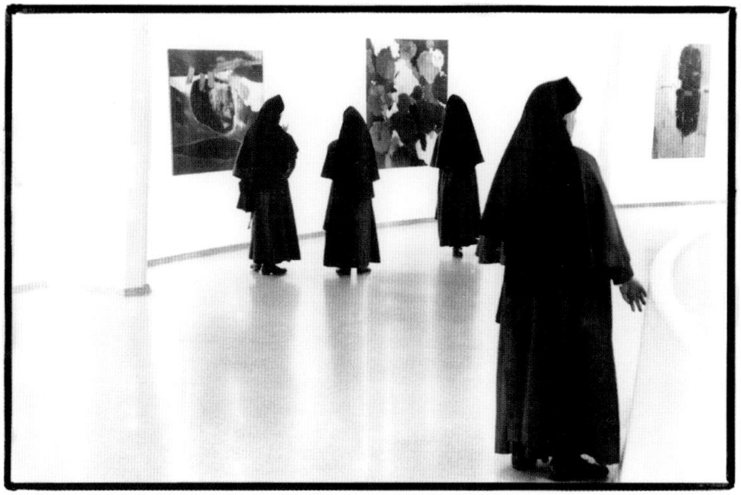

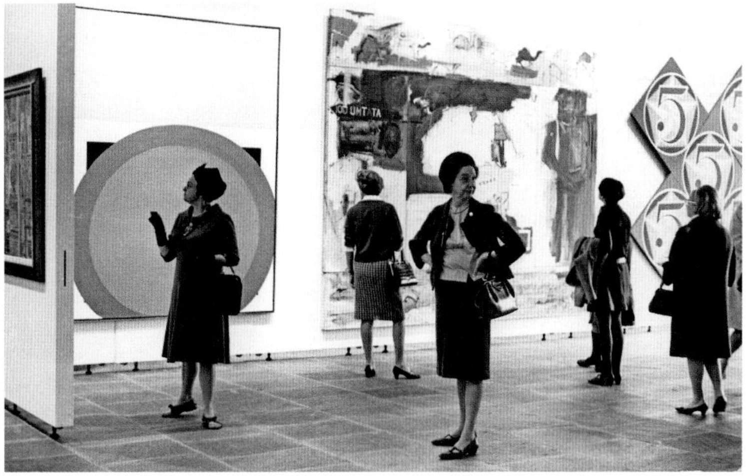

Neil Libbert,
The Whitney, 1960

that she is beautiful, whilst the older woman's blurred face, cigarette firmly in place, leaves little doubt as to her age and class. Again, Libbert records typical New York sights, imbued with his own subtle irony.

In *Lower East Side*, 1964 (p. 94) Libbert presents the viewer with a hugely complex scene – a well-dressed boy is having his photograph taken by a street photographer. His mother, still holding the paper bag that the boy's new gun came in, is advising him as to how to pose, whilst the photographer's assistant (or is he the boy's father?) stands by idly chewing his thumb. In the foreground corner a young child stares up at the camera whilst being tugged away by the hand of a hurrying adult. The drama is set next to a Kosher food shop advertising *Steaks*, *Chops* and *Catering* in the window, which is also painted with Hebrew lettering. The boy poses like a gangster, one hand caressing his belly and the other brandishing his new gun. His mother's anxious expression suggests how spoilt he is, as we are drawn into the theatre of the moment. We feel the tension as the photographer goes underneath his cloth to take the photograph, looking slightly comic as his rear end sticks out beyond the edges of the frame. The composition, which at first appears to be full of action, is held around a series of parallel diagonals – the gun, the paper bag, the photographer's back, and in the other direction, the protagonists' shadows. It is a picture that both encapsulates New York and also the histories that have been discussed in this essay – the street photographer, who could be Jewish, has been photographed in a Jewish neighbourhood by another outsider, himself a Jew. Thus continuing the thread that links the itinerant Jewish photographers of the nineteenth century, via the émigrés of the twentieth century to the photographers discussed here, whose journeys to new cities have enabled them to photograph without prejudice and to see with fresh eyes.

[1] Sarah MacDougall and Rachel Dickson, Eds., *Out of Chaos. Ben Uri: 100 Years in London* (London: Ben Uri, 2015).

[2] Dorothy Bohm is one of the first photographers whose work has entered the Ben Uri collection. Ibid., cat. no. 53.

[3] The debate continues to this day. See, for example, Sean O'Hagan, 'Photography is Art and Always Will Be', *The Guardian*, 11 December 2014.

[4] Sara Blair, 'Jewish America Through the Lens', *Michigan Quarterly Review*, Vol. XLII, No. 1 (Winter, 2003), pp. 113–34.

[5] Michael Berkowitz, *Jews and Photography in Britain* (Austin: University of Texas Press, 2015), p. 2.

[6] Nissan N. Perez, *Displaced Visions: Émigré Photographers of the 20th Century* (Jerusalem: Israel Museum, 2013).

[7] Allan Douglass Coleman, 'No Pictures: Some Thoughts on Jews in Photography' (1998), http://www.nearbycafe.com/adc/adcmenu/readings/jews.html, accessed on 14/3/16

[8] Michael Omasta, Brigitte Mayr and Ursula Seeber, Eds., *Wolf Suschitzky Photos* (Vienna: Synema, 2006), p. 184.

[9] Berkowitz, *Jews and Photography*, p. 75.

[10] Julia Winckler, 'The Photography of Wolfgang Suschitzky', in *London Independent Photography*, No. 18 (Winter, 2004/5), p. 5.

[11] Dervla Murphy, 'Introduction', in *Down and Out in London and Paris*, by George Orwell (London: Penguin Books, 2001), p. xiii.

[12] Winckler, *The Photography of Wolfgang Suschitzky*, p. 7.

[13] Omasta, *Wolf Suschitzky Photos*, p. 184.

[14] Mass-Observation Archive: Topic Collections, 43 'Propaganda and Morale 1939–1944', Box 5F 'Ministry of Information Exhibitions 1940–44', 'Propaganda Exhibitions 1942–44'. The archive is housed at the University of Sussex.

[15] Janina Struk, *Photographing the Holocaust: Interpretations of the Evidence* (London and New York: I.B. Tauris & Co. Ltd., 2004), pp. 55–6.

[16] Mark Haworth-Booth, Françoise Reynaud and Lynne Woolfson, *Un amour de Paris: photographs by / photographies de Dorothy Bohm* (Paris: Paris-Musées, 2005).

[17] Julian Stallabrass, *Paris Pictured* (London: Royal Academy of Arts, 2002), pp. 9–11.

[18] Richard D. Lyons, 'Obituary: Frederick A. Praeger Dies at 78; Published Books on Communism', *New York Times*, 5 June 1994.

[19] Press Release for *New Documents*, released by the Museum of Modern Art, on 28 February, 1967. The text continues: 'What is held in common is the belief that the world is worth looking at, and the courage to look at it without theorizing.'

[20] Of his photograph *Brixton on Fire*, Libbert said 'This was reminiscent of the Harlem race riots in 1964, which I also photographed. So I'd seen this scene before – and it was rather frightening.' Anonymous compiler and interviewer, 'Brixton riots – in pictures', *The Observer*, 10 April, 2011, http://www.theguardian.com/uk/gallery/2011/apr/10/police-race, accessed on 14/4/16.

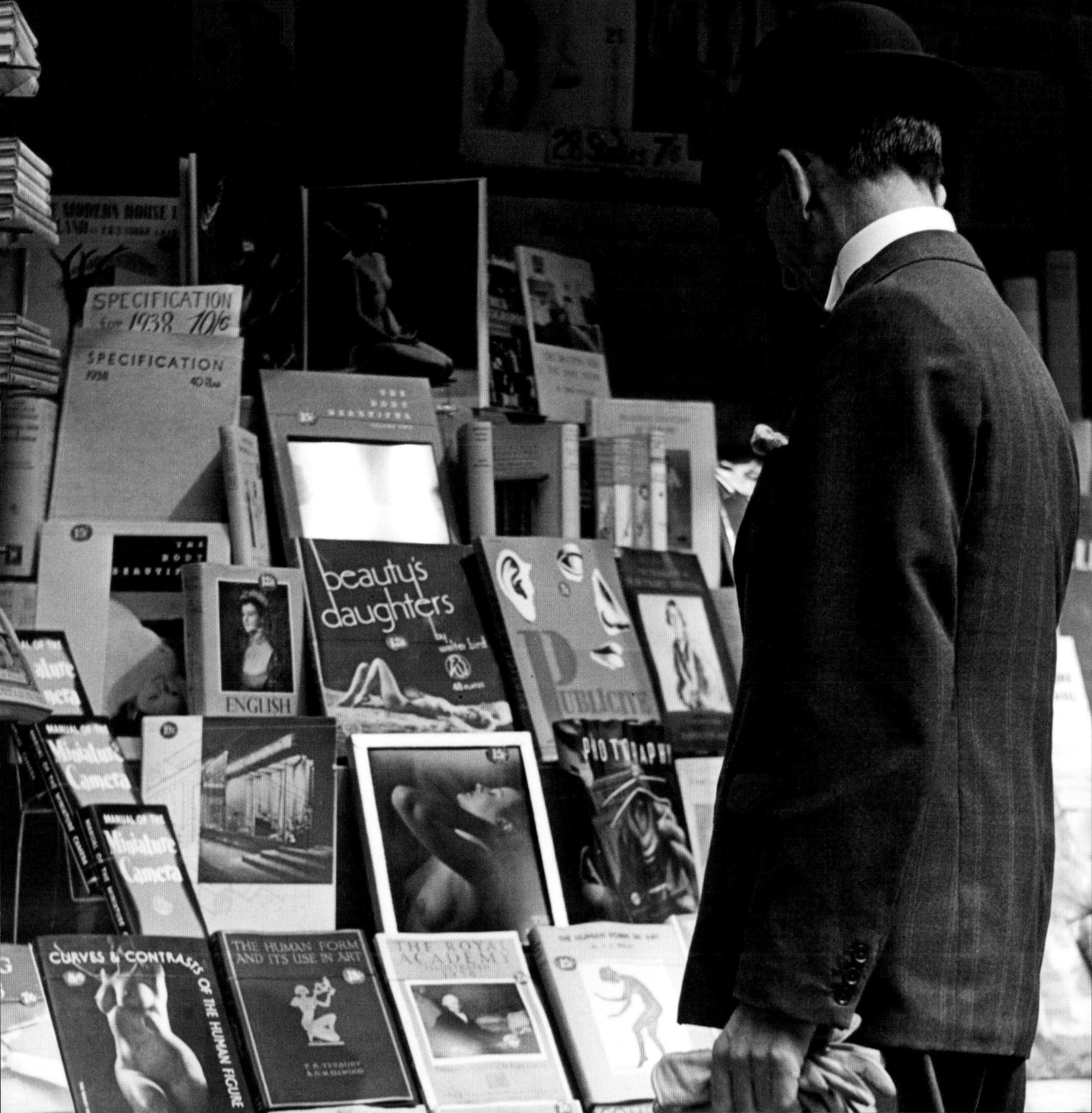
SPECIFICATION
1938 10/6
SPECIFICATION
beauty's daughters
ENGLISH
Miniature Camera
Miniature Camera
CURVES & CONTRASTS OF THE HUMAN FIGURE
THE HUMAN FORM AND ITS USE IN ART
THE ROYAL ACADEMY

Wolf Suschitzky
London

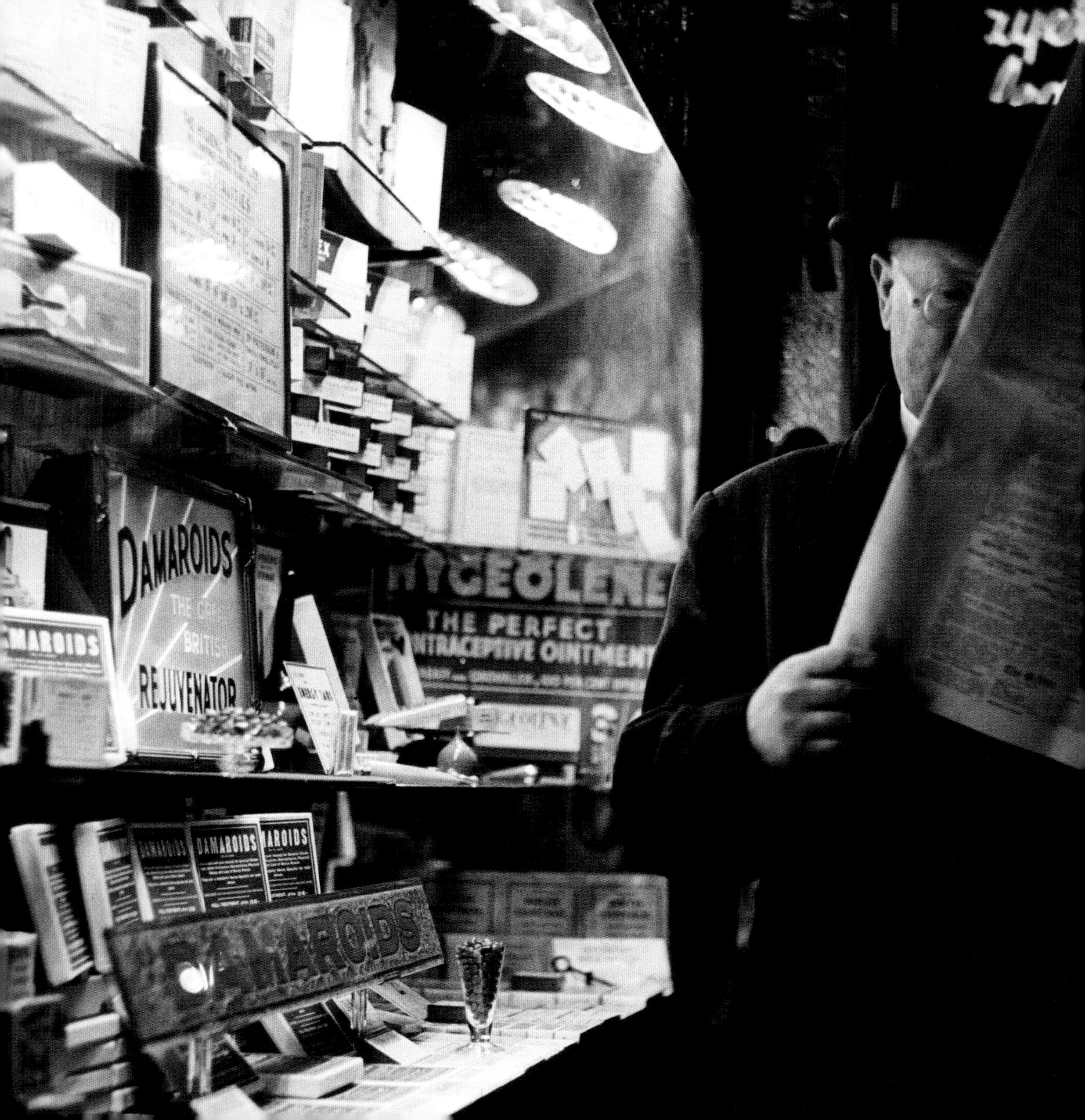
DAMAROIDS
BRITISH
REJUVENATOR
MAROIDS
ENERGY TABS
THE PERFECT
DAMAROIDS
DAMAROIDS
MAROIDS
MAROIDS

Wolf Suschitzky
In conversation with Zelda Cheatle

It is 3.00pm and I am standing on the doorstep of Wolf Suschitzky's home in Maida Vale, in the rain.

A disembodied voice greets me from above, through the intercom. Wolf is waiting to greet me as I step out of the lift.

The last time I saw Wolf it was his 103rd birthday and we were gathered in the sunny garden, his family having made a wondrous summer lunch.

I am here today to talk to Wolf about his forthcoming exhibition at Ben Uri, which will focus on cities – London, Paris and New York.

Wolf's allocation in the exhibition is clearly London – as he shows me the portfolio that Katy Barron has selected from all his London pictures.

I am very familiar with the pictures, so it is a great pleasure to sit with Wolf and go through them one by one. Wolf retains his quiet and courteous manner; he is interested in people and life. We begin to go through the pictures.

Zelda Cheatle: What was happening in photography when you arrived in London?

Wolf Suschitzky: London seemed very far behind, I came with the knowledge of German realism and the London scene was dominated by the Royal Photographic Society Annual Salon. The photographs were all emulating paintings, which I did not really like.

ZC: So began your odyssey to Charing Cross Road from 1934 to 1939. Because of leaving your father's bookshop in Vienna, you were drawn to Charing Cross Road?

WS: Yes, I used to enjoy all the bookshops. Now it's all cafés and hairdressers.

ZC: Did London seem grubby and dark after the clean air of Vienna?

WS: Yes, it was darker – but I sought out the dark and the grubby. I liked to find the other side of London. I liked to go to the East End and see the architecture, the homes, life on the streets, or the docks and study the life of the river and Port of London.

ZC: Did anybody ever question you about what you were doing?

WS: Many times people would come up to me and ask if I was photographing for the *Daily Mirror*.

ZC: But you never worked for the *Daily Mirror*?

WS: No, but it was the paper best known in the East End.

ZC: Were you ever in *Picture Post*? As this was a popular way of looking at pictures – photographs – during this era.

WS: I had a cover once and some pictures in *Picture Post*, but I was in *Illustrated London News* much more often, which was a competitor. I had breakfast with Sir Tom Hopkinson once and he told me he liked my photographs but that I was not a photojournalist.

ZC: That is true, interesting he could see it so succinctly. I think of you as a quiet observer rather than making bold statements.

WS: I like that thought. I was busy making films a lot of the time.

ZC: I cannot imagine you elbowing people out of the way either, you are much too well mannered.

WS: It's not my nature. Look at that picture on the wall. [Wolf points to *Guy the Gorilla*.] He is very intelligent.

ZC: I can tell that he had the sum of you in those eyes. You were drawn to zoology weren't you?

WS: Yes – I enjoy photographing animals. I would have liked to be a zoologist.

ZC: Back to Charing Cross Road in the 1930s. This one is great as it has number 84 Charing Cross Road in it, a young tree and an air of mystery.

WS: Yes – and the sapling tree in that picture is now a big tree that reaches up to the third storey on Charing Cross Road.

ZC: The Foyles reader, such a great advertisement for Foyles.

WS: I offered it to them once, but they were not interested.

ZC: More fool them! Other people have enjoyed it greatly.

WS: The wooden blocks that you see them laying beneath the tarmac is how Charing Cross Road was constructed. It was thought to be better for horses' hooves.

ZC: Many of the photographs are in the West End, but where did you first live in London?

WS: I lived in Brixton with my sister Edith Tudor Hart. Her husband was a doctor who bought a practice in Brixton. I remember the market by the railway line, and Electric Avenue where electricity first came to London.

ZC: I did not know you started as a south Londoner. You must come back to visit. How do you think London has changed?

WS: In my pictures there are hardly any cars, now there are cars everywhere. In Paris it's the same, a motorway next to the Seine – on both sides. It's almost impossible to photograph without cars these days.

ZC: Do you like London?

WS: I think it has changed in my years here. Now I walk down Edgware Road and hardly hear any English spoken.

ZC: I think that is the same in many cities now – cities get bigger all the time. Migration is constant. But London still feels a safe city to live in.

WS: We did not have so many knife attacks before.

ZC: I have just come back from the United Arab Emirates. It feels very good to be back in London where women are equal.

WS: Yes, I am very glad I live in London.

Wolf decides it's time for tea and makes a very fine Lady Grey. Heather, Wolf's partner, arrived back from a visit to Sir John Soane's Museum and we three had tea together. Heather was very happy to have seen the museum and especially the paintings she had remembered from a visit made many years previously. Wolf made fresh tea and we had some very nice biscuits!

24 March 2016

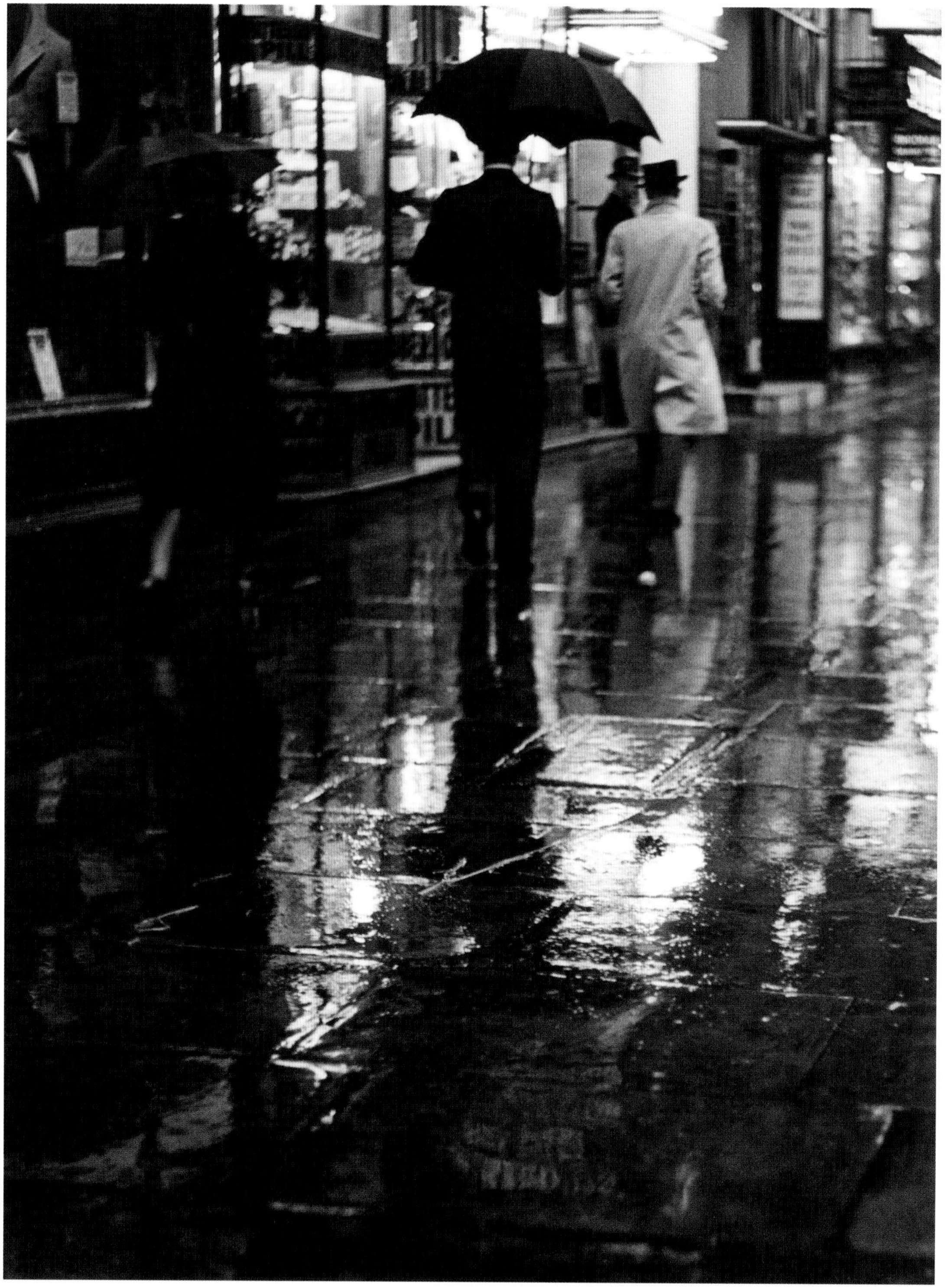

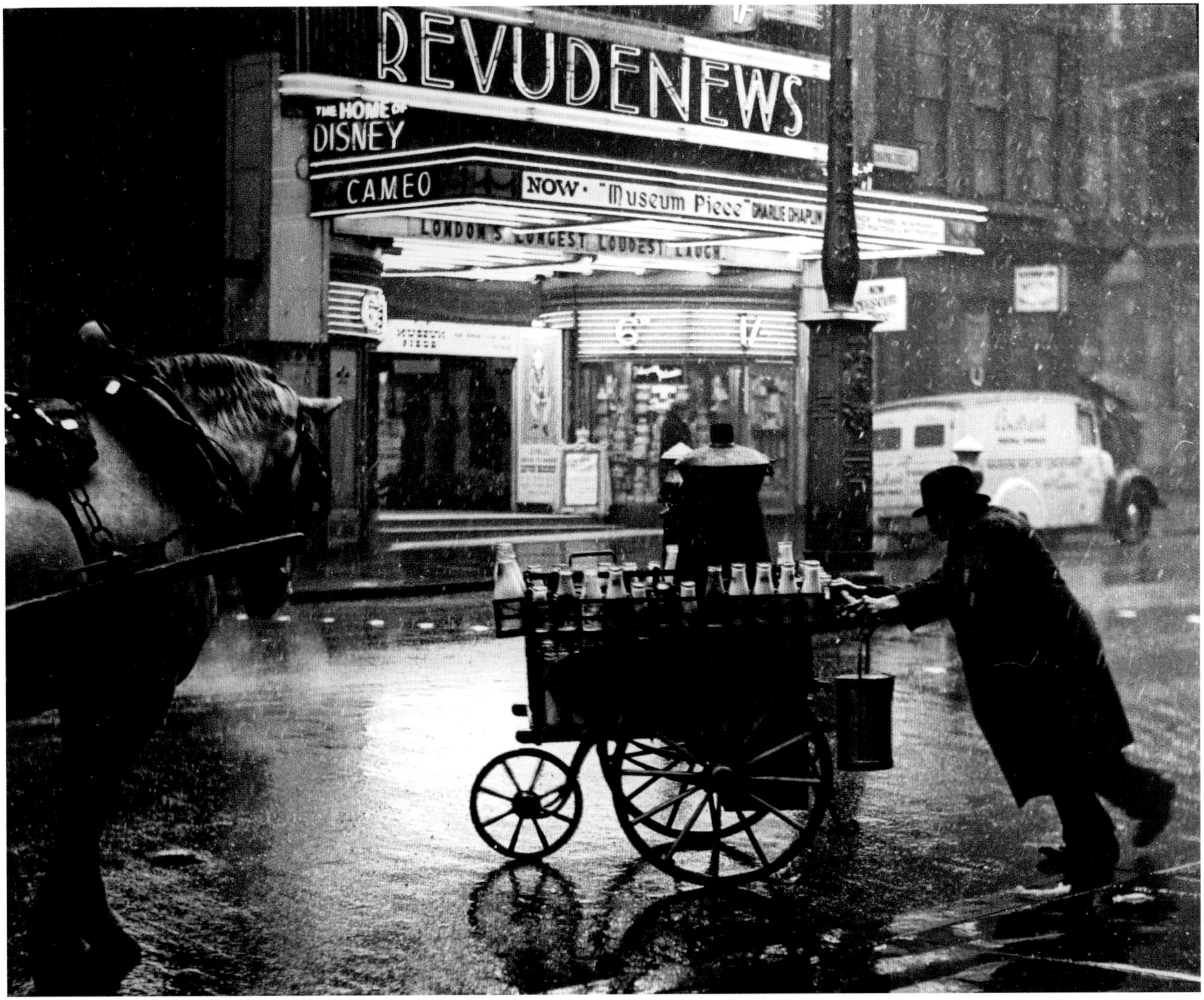
REVUDENEWS
THE HOME OF
DISNEY
CAMEO
NOW · "Museum Piece" CHARLIE CHAPLIN
LONDON'S LONGEST LOUDEST LAUGH

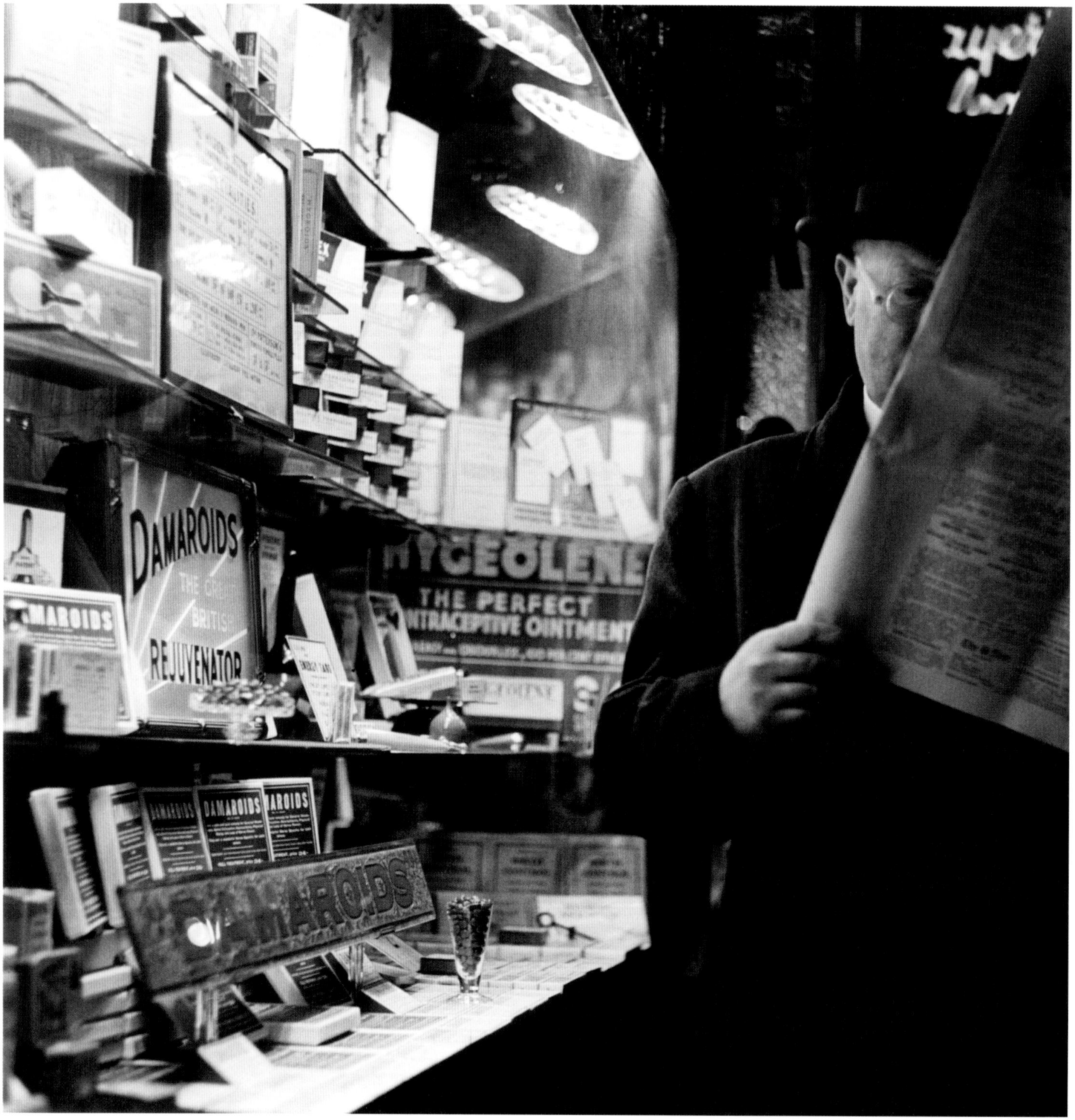
DAMAROIDS
REJUVENATOR
THE PERFECT
DAMAROIDS

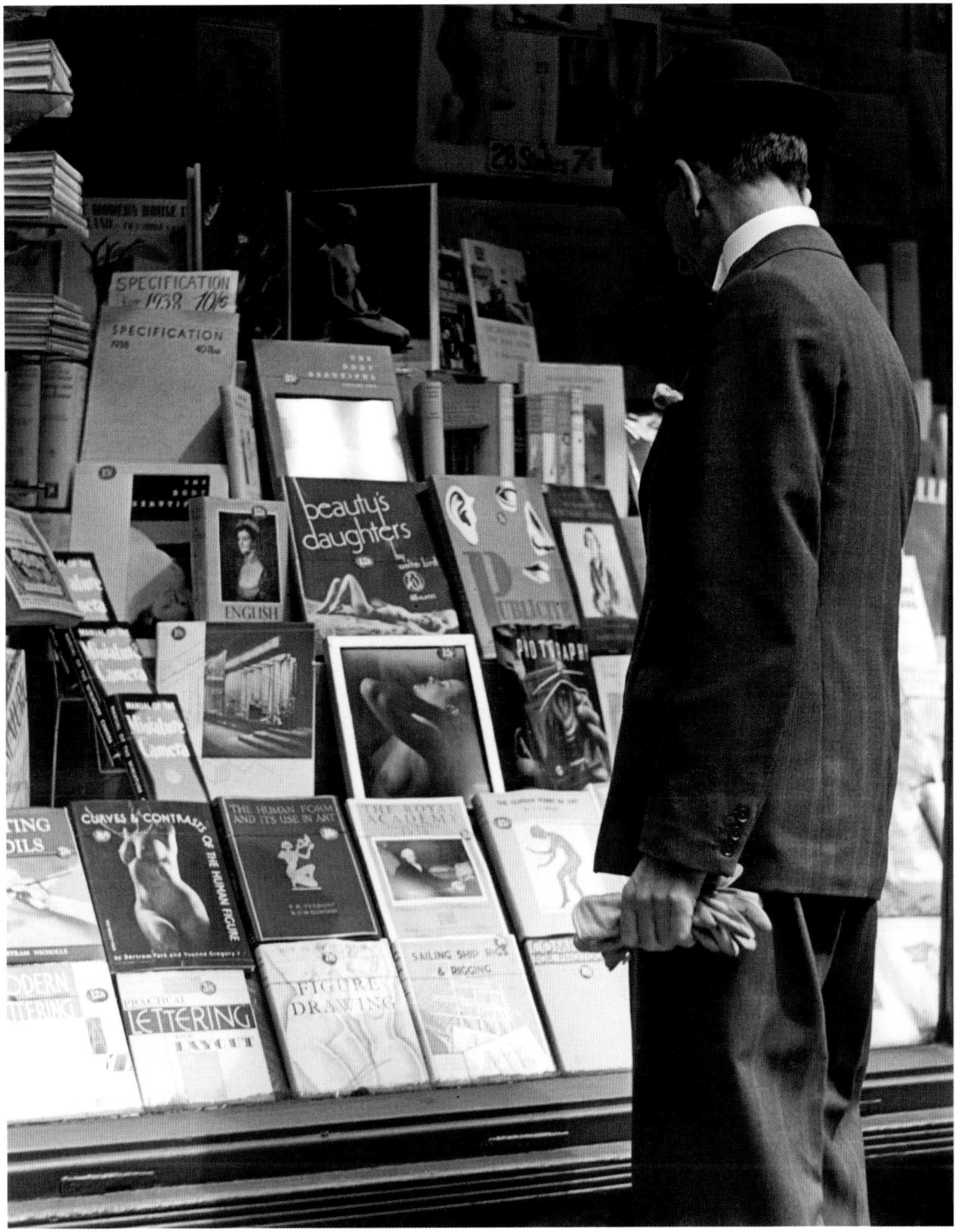
SPECIFICATION
1938 10/6
SPECIFICATION
1938
beauty's daughters
ENGLISH
CURVES & CONTRASTS OF THE HUMAN FIGURE
THE HUMAN FORM AND ITS USE IN ART
SAILING SHIP RIGS & RIGGING
FIGURE DRAWING
PRACTICAL LETTERING AND LAYOUT

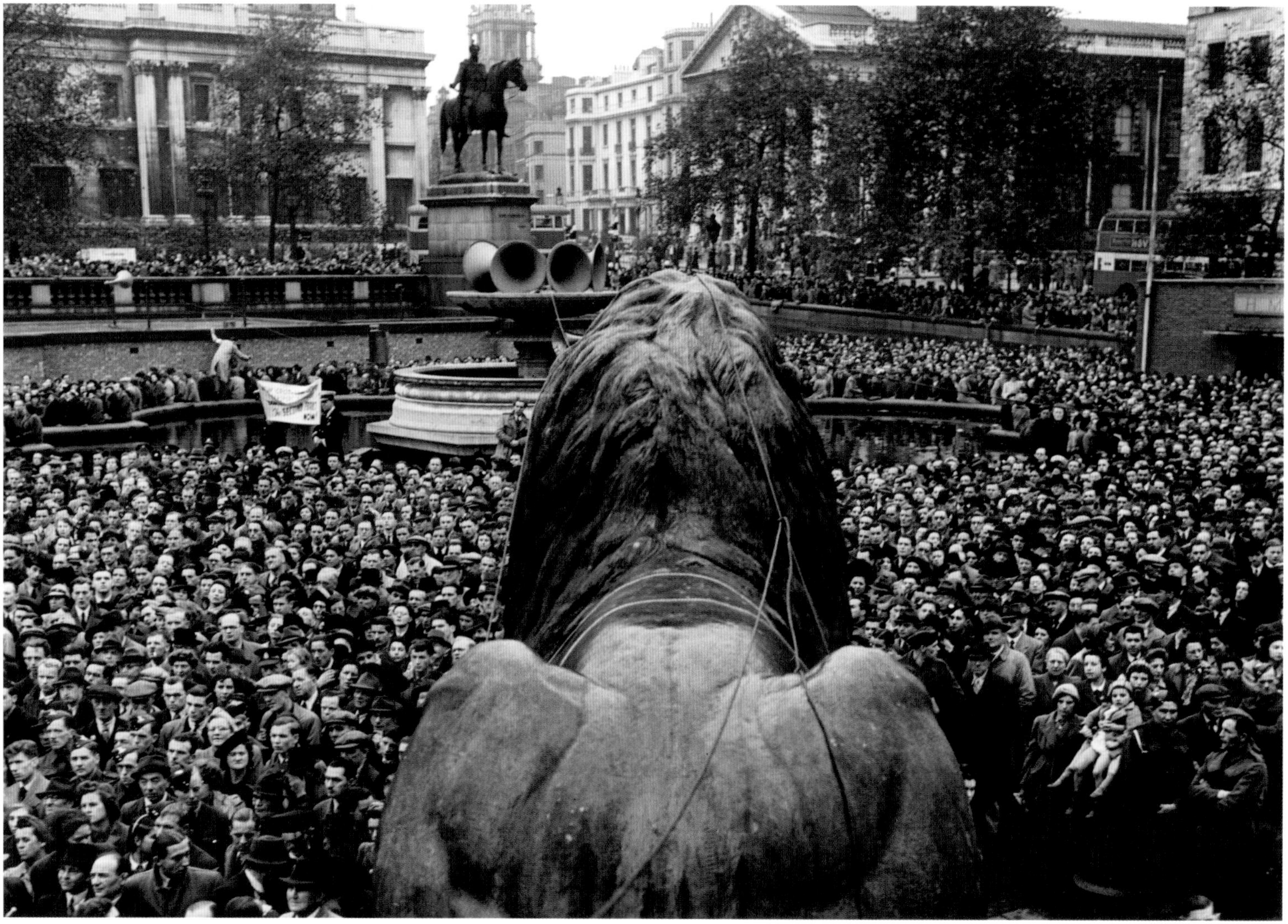

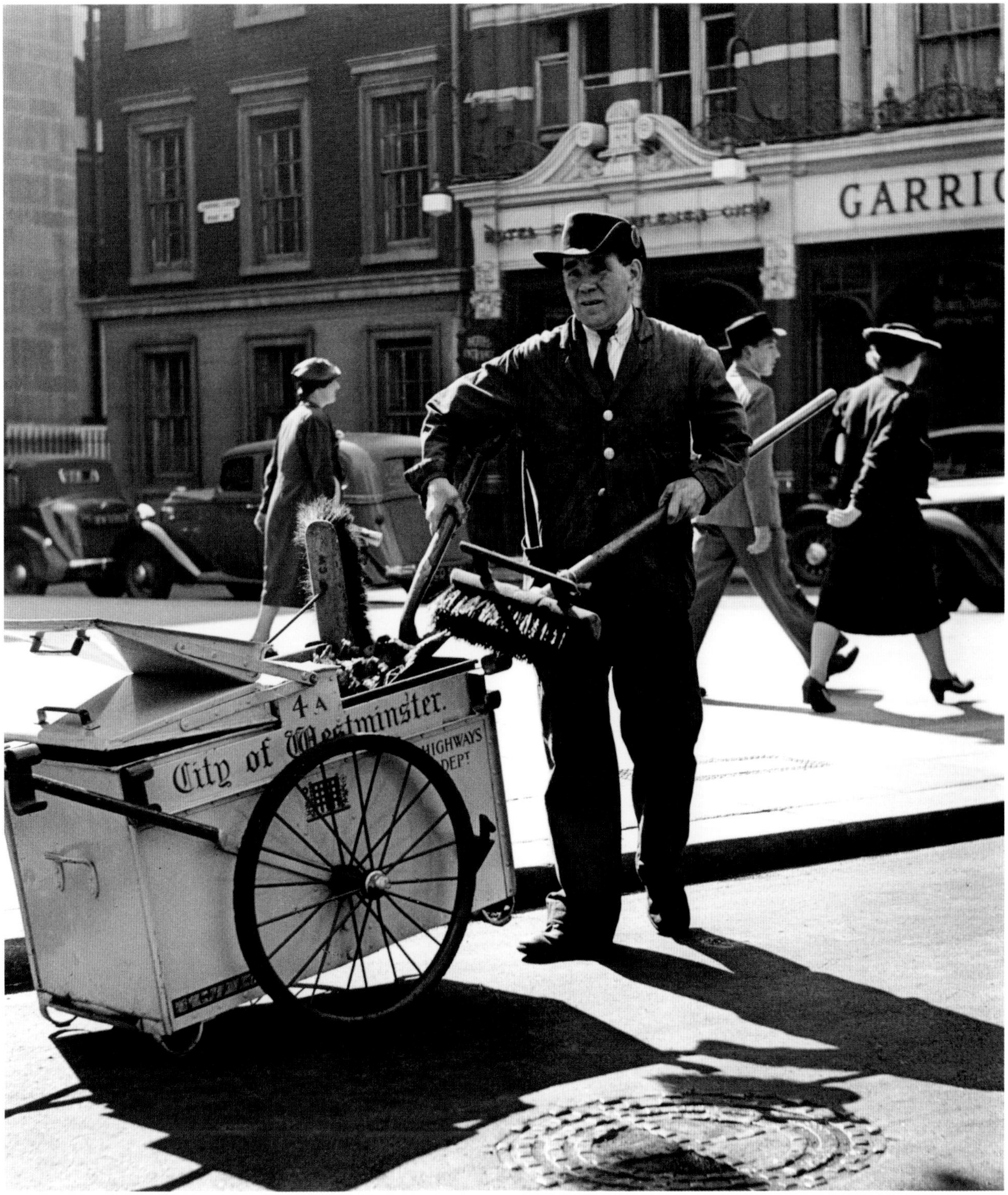
GARRIC
4 A
City of Westminster.
HIGHWAYS
DEPT

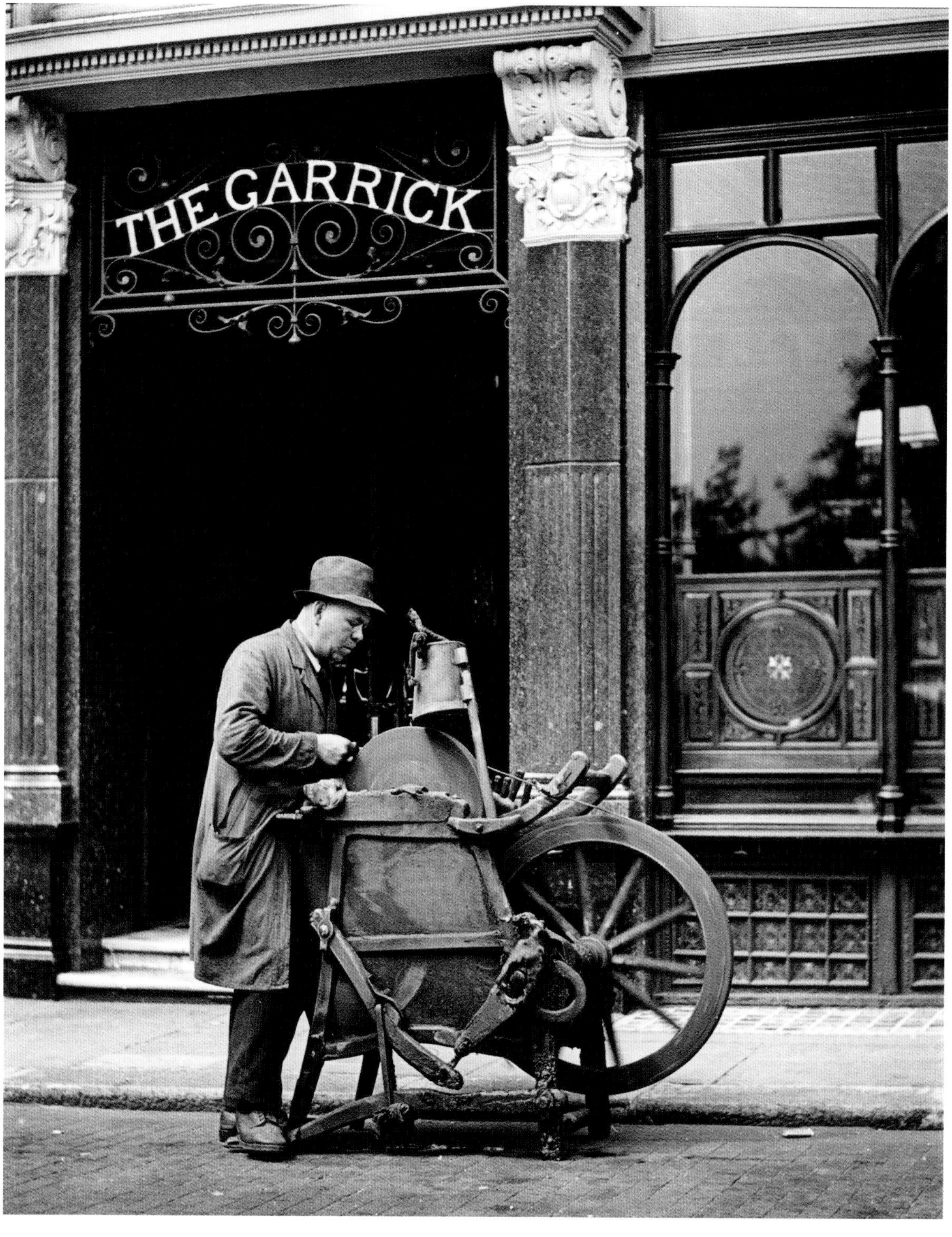
THE GARRICK

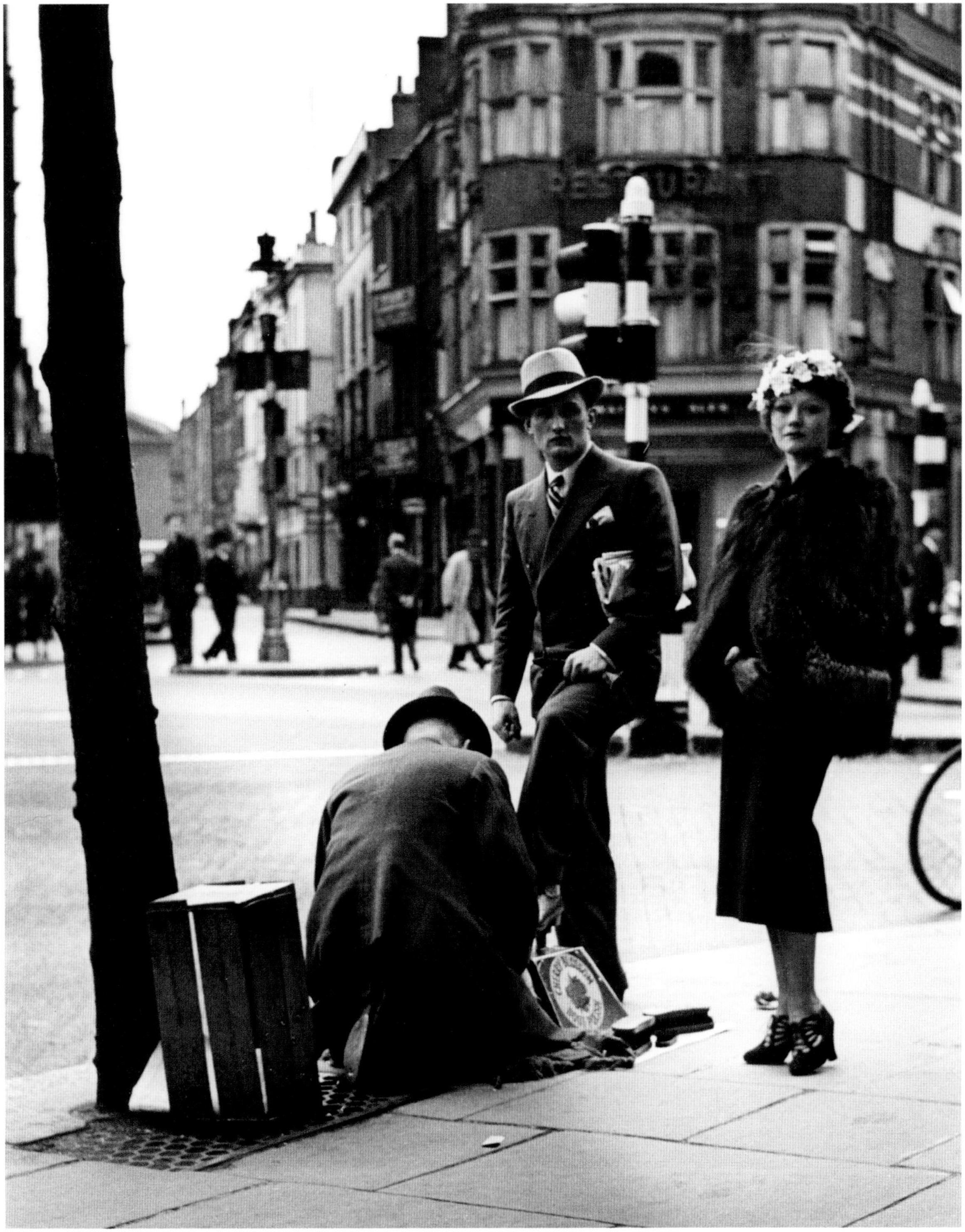

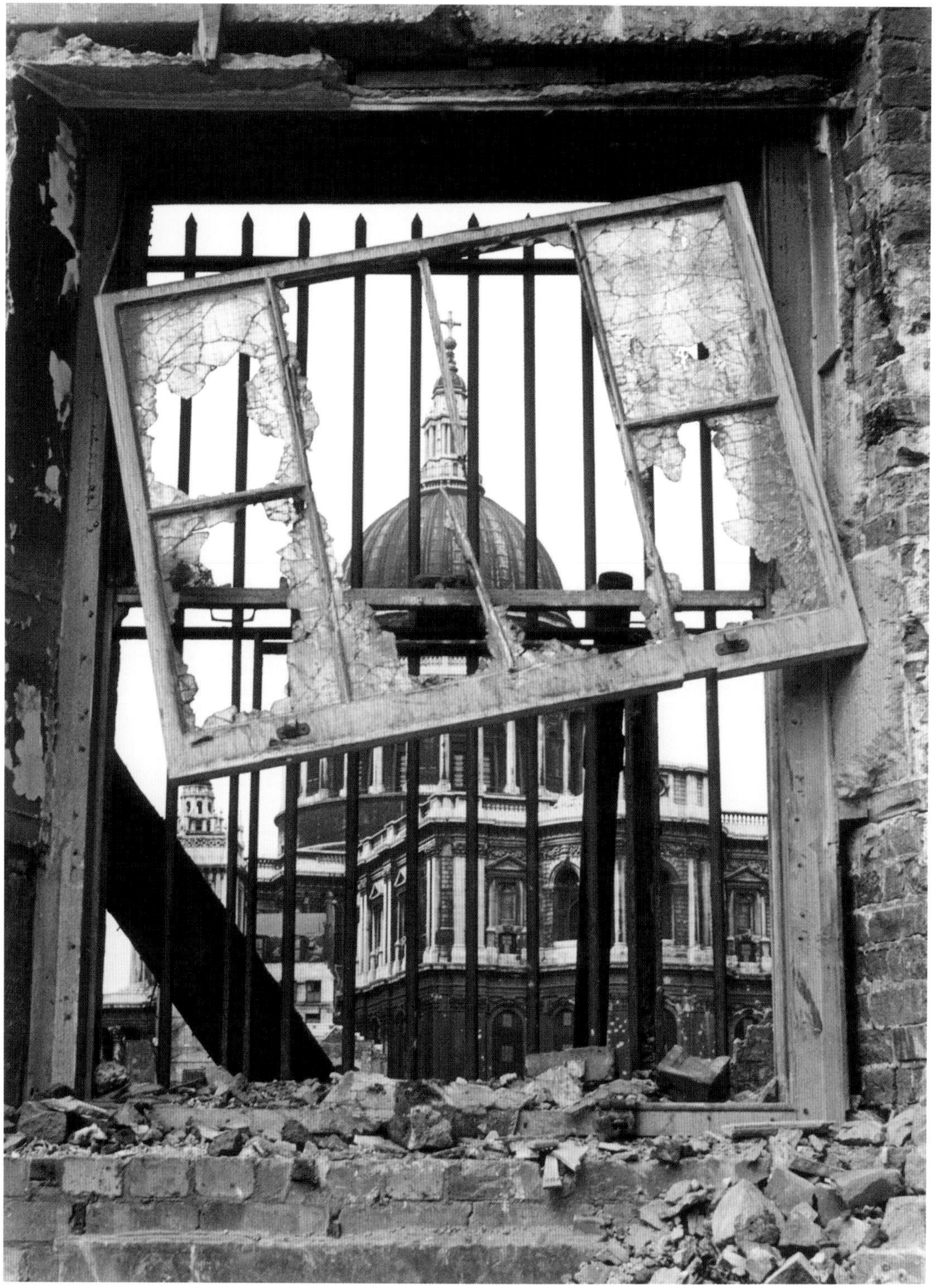

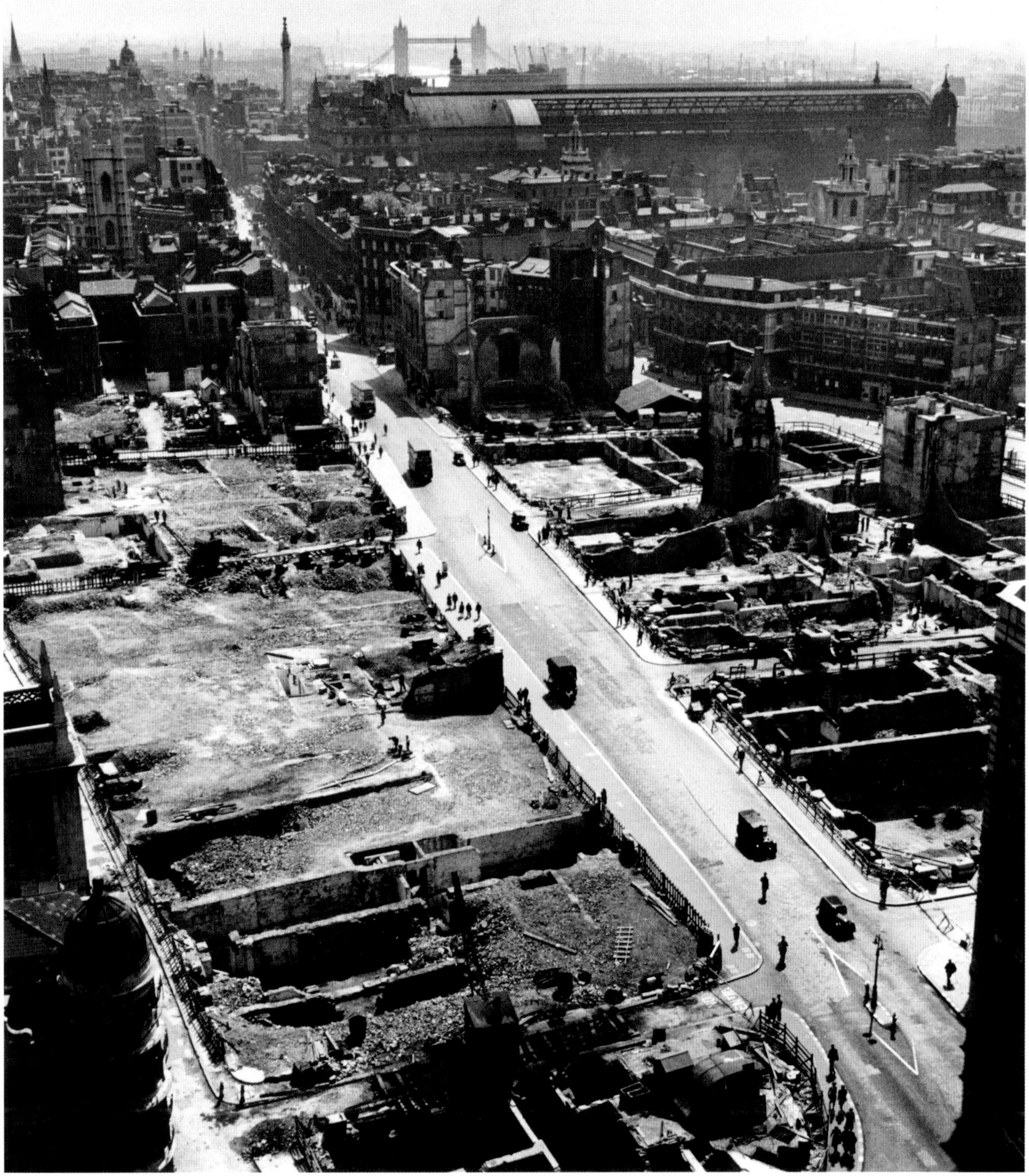

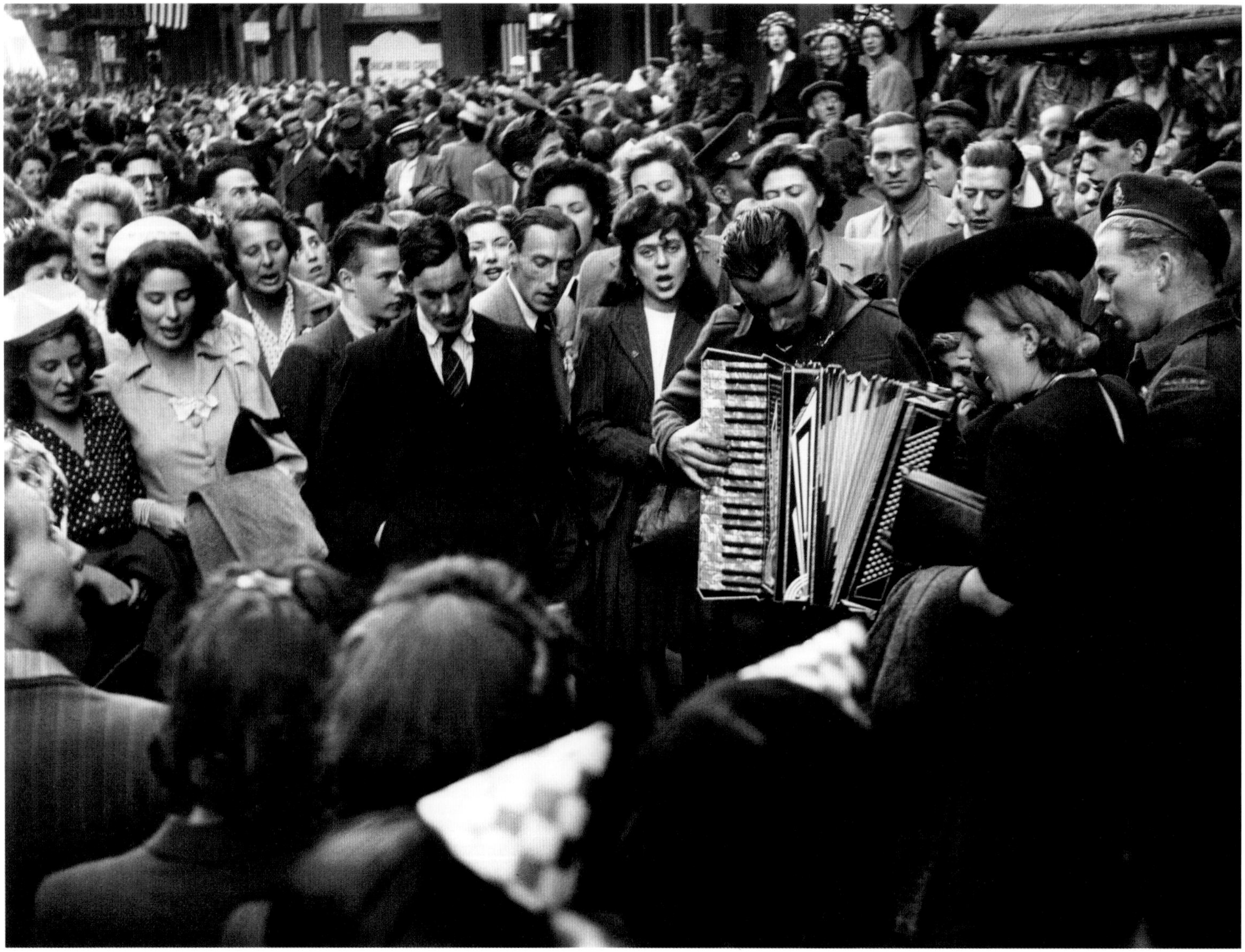

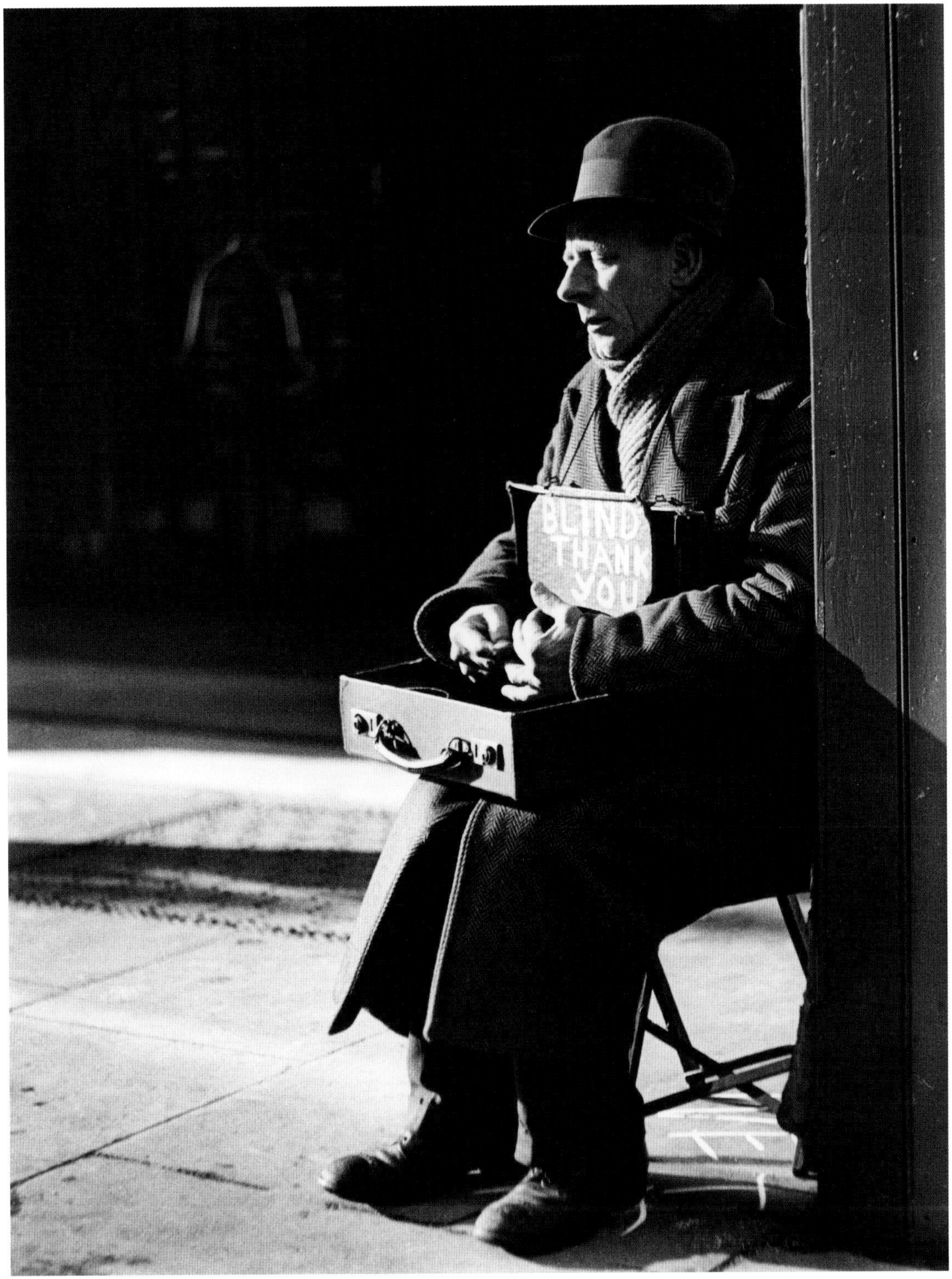
BLIND
THANK
YOU

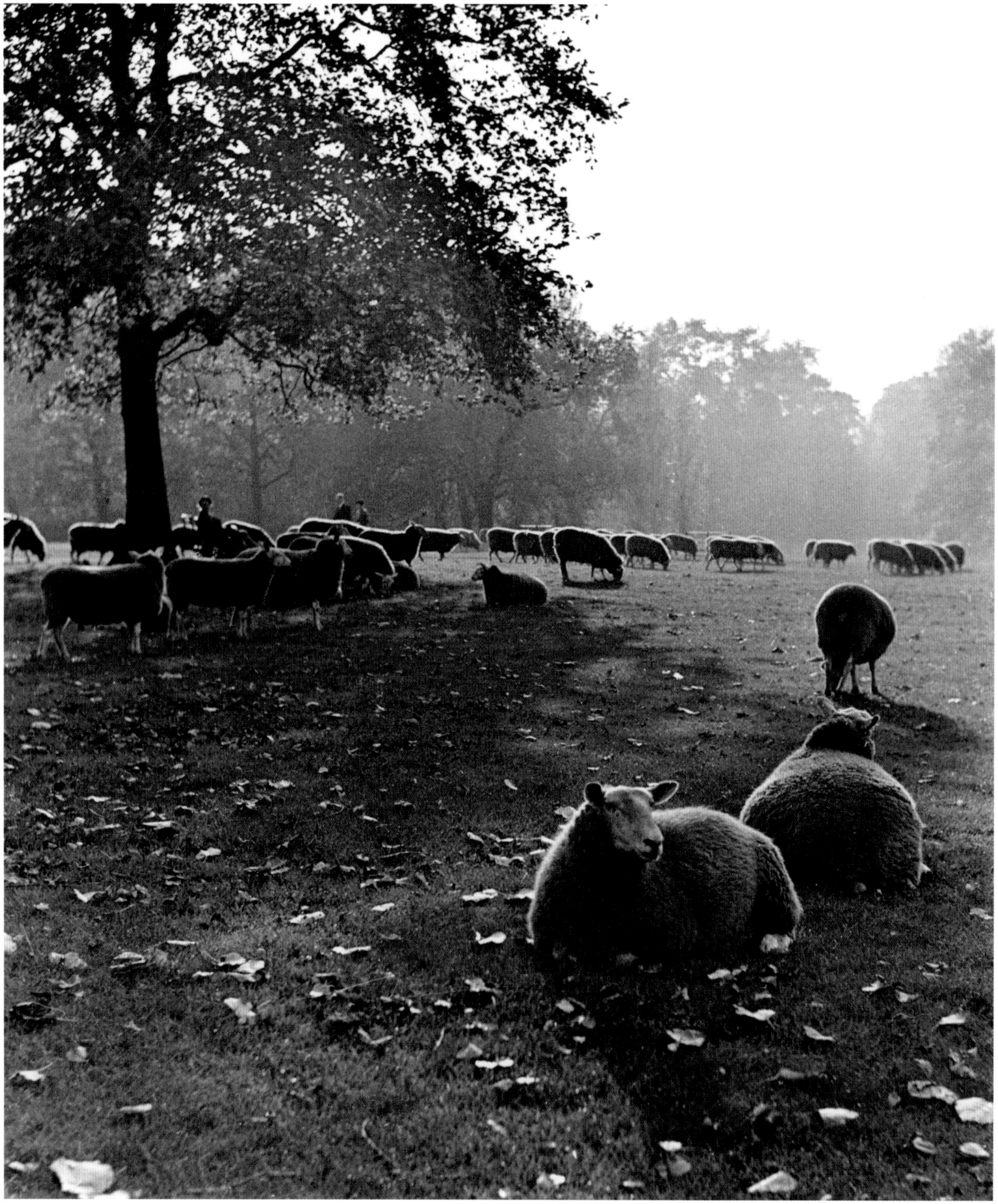

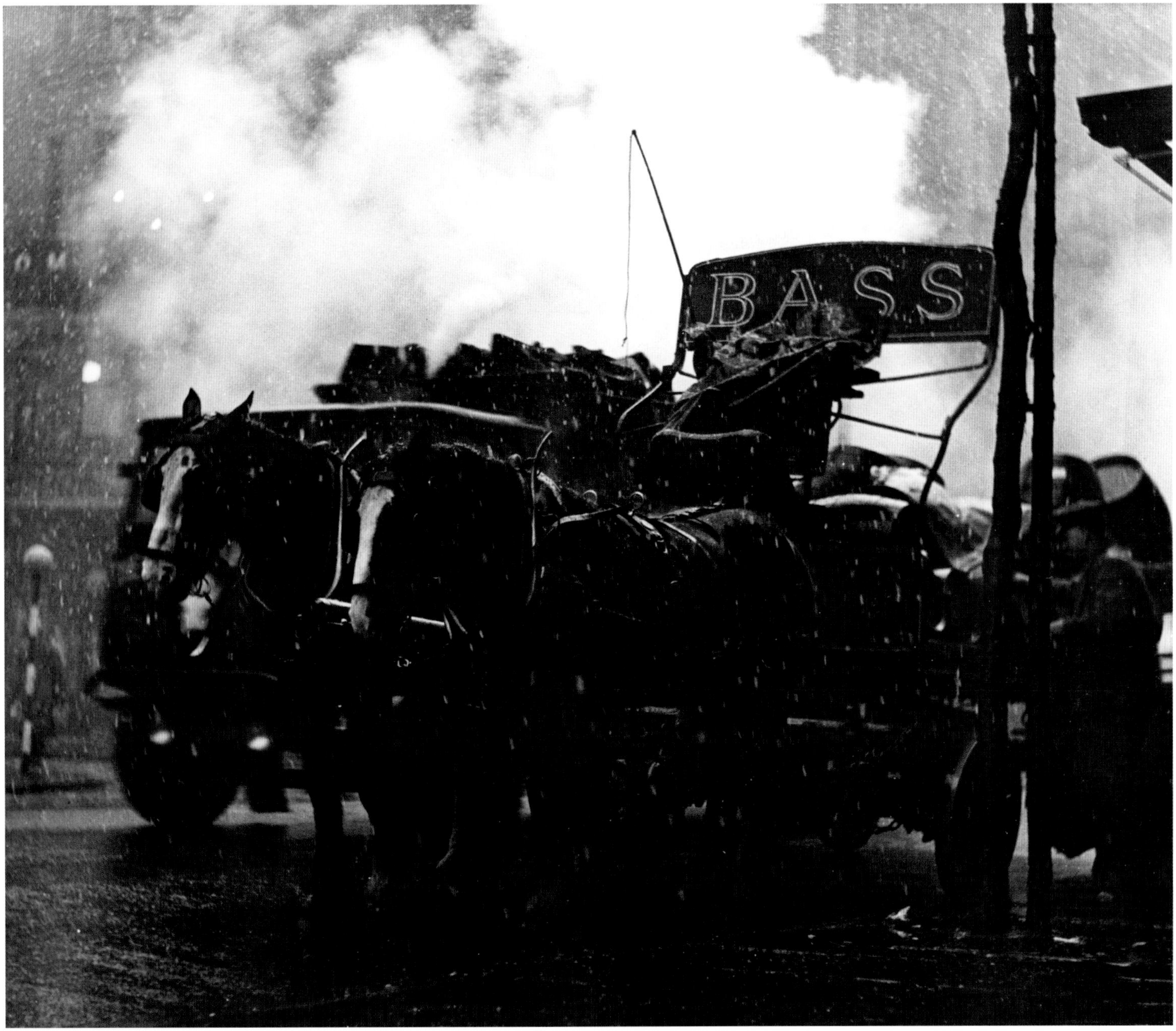
BASS

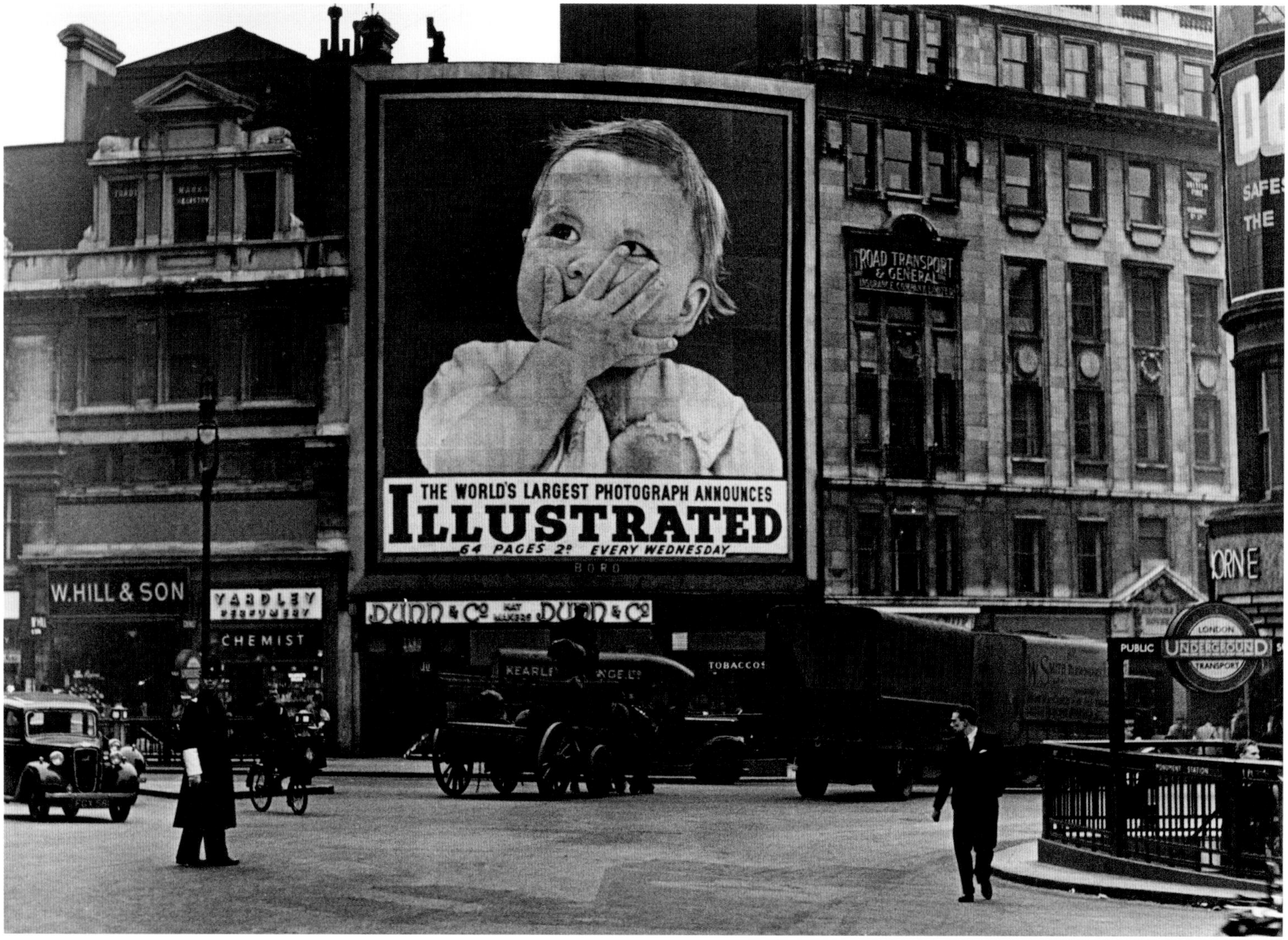
THE WORLD'S LARGEST PHOTOGRAPH ANNOUNCES
ILLUSTRATED
64 PAGES 2D EVERY WEDNESDAY
W.HILL & SON
YARDLEY
CHEMIST
DUNN & Co
DUNN & Co
ROAD TRANSPORT & GENERAL
TOBACCOS
PUBLIC
LONDON
UNDERGROUND
TRANSPORT

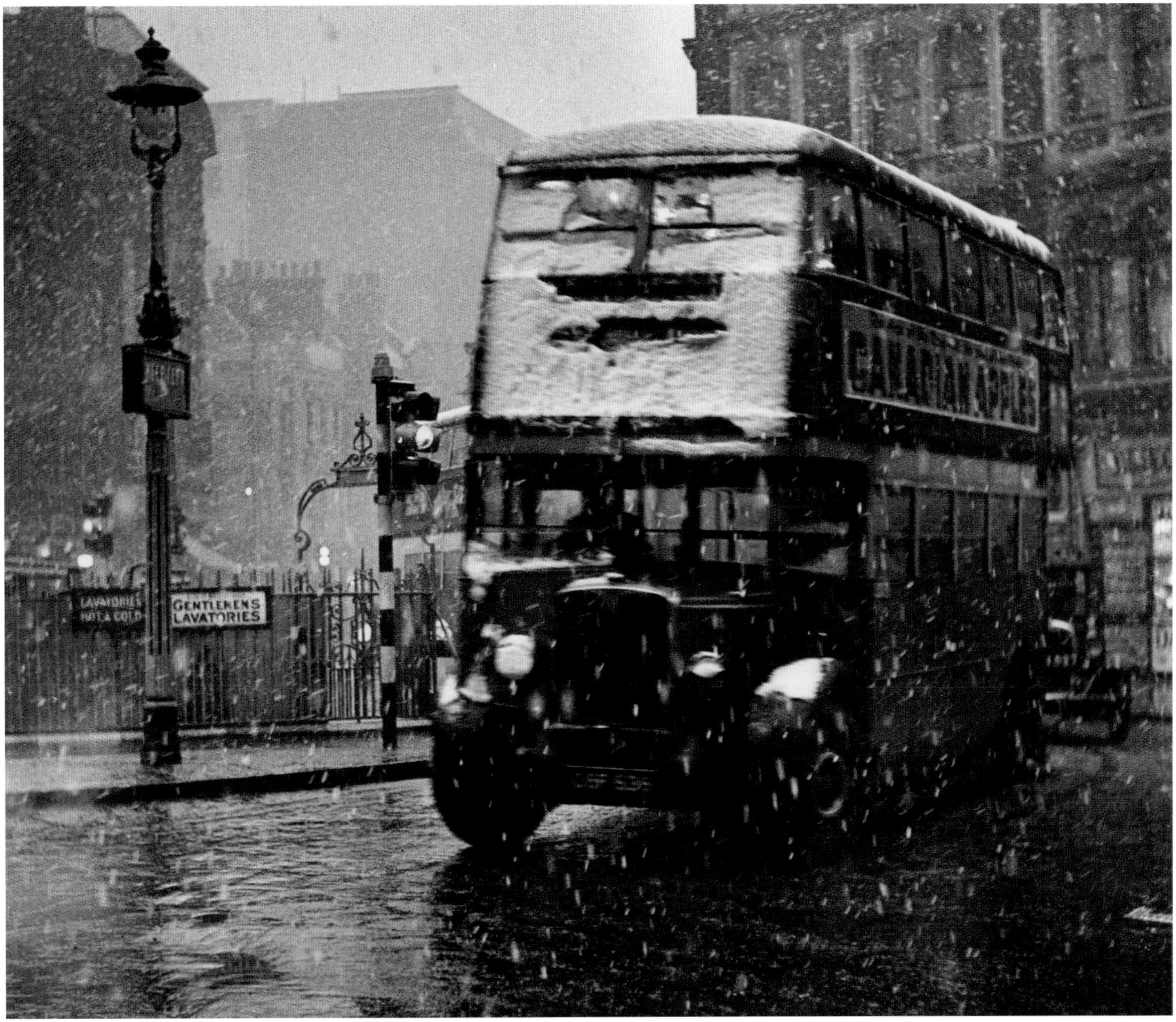
GENTLEMENS
LAVATORIES
CANADIAN APPLES

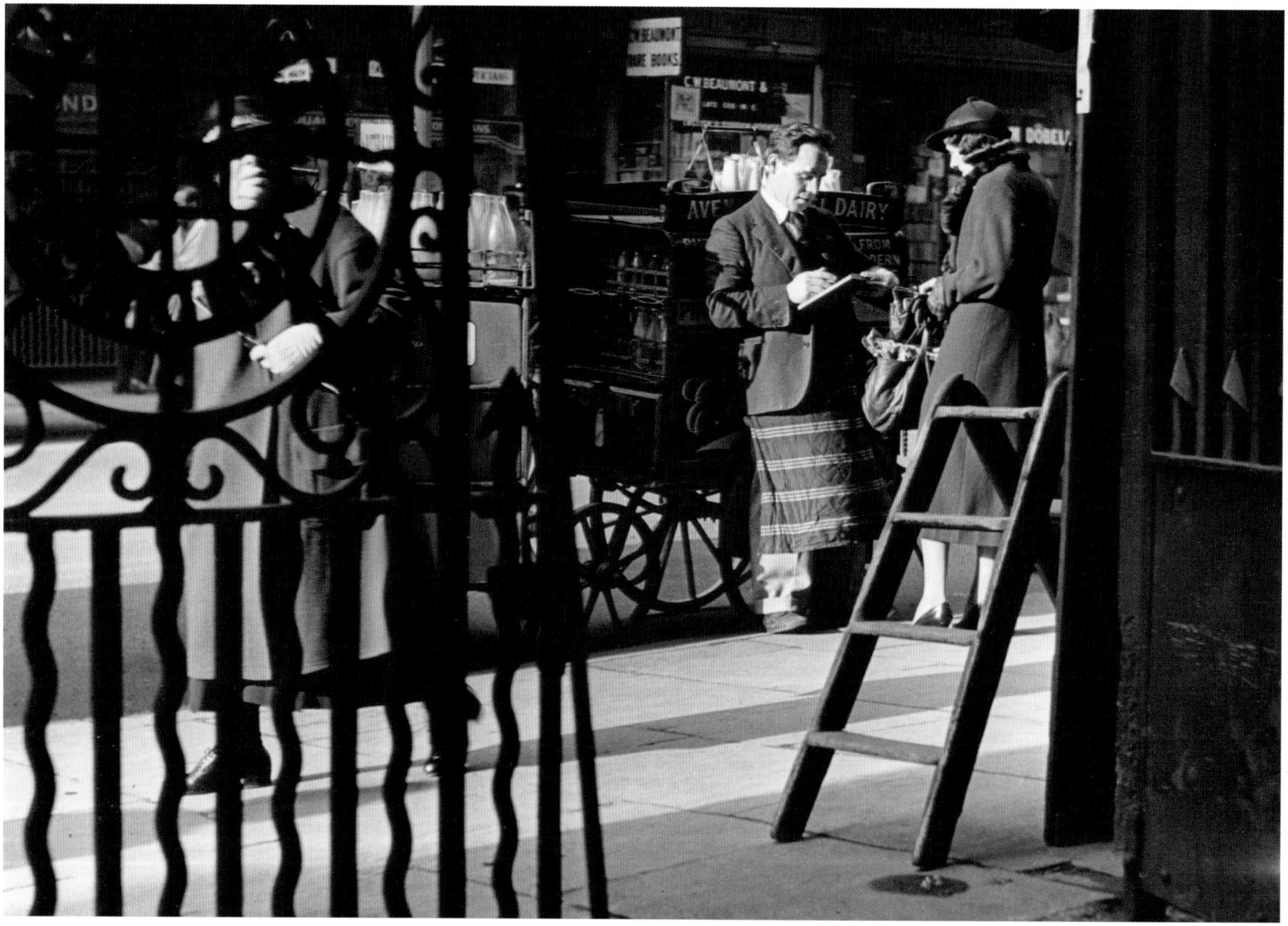
RARE BOOKS
C.W BEAUMONT &
DAIRY
FROM

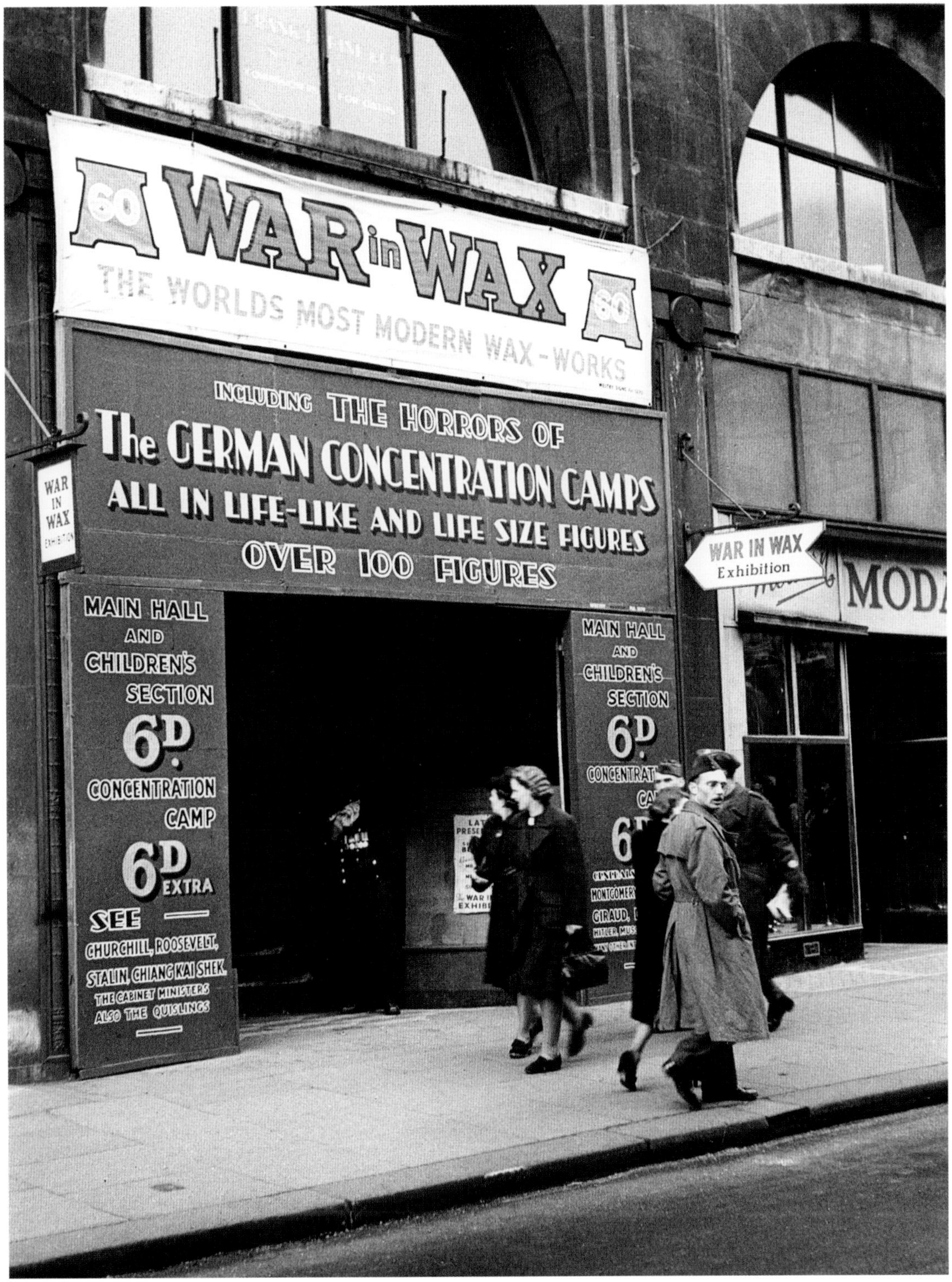
WAR in WAX
60
THE WORLDS MOST MODERN WAX-WORKS
INCLUDING THE HORRORS OF
The GERMAN CONCENTRATION CAMPS
ALL IN LIFE-LIKE AND LIFE SIZE FIGURES
OVER 100 FIGURES
WAR IN WAX EXHIBITION
WAR IN WAX Exhibition
MAIN HALL AND CHILDREN'S SECTION 6D.
CONCENTRATION CAMP 6D EXTRA
SEE
CHURCHILL, ROOSEVELT, STALIN, CHIANG KAI SHEK, THE CABINET MINISTERS ALSO THE QUISLINGS
MAIN HALL AND CHILDREN'S SECTION 6D
MODA

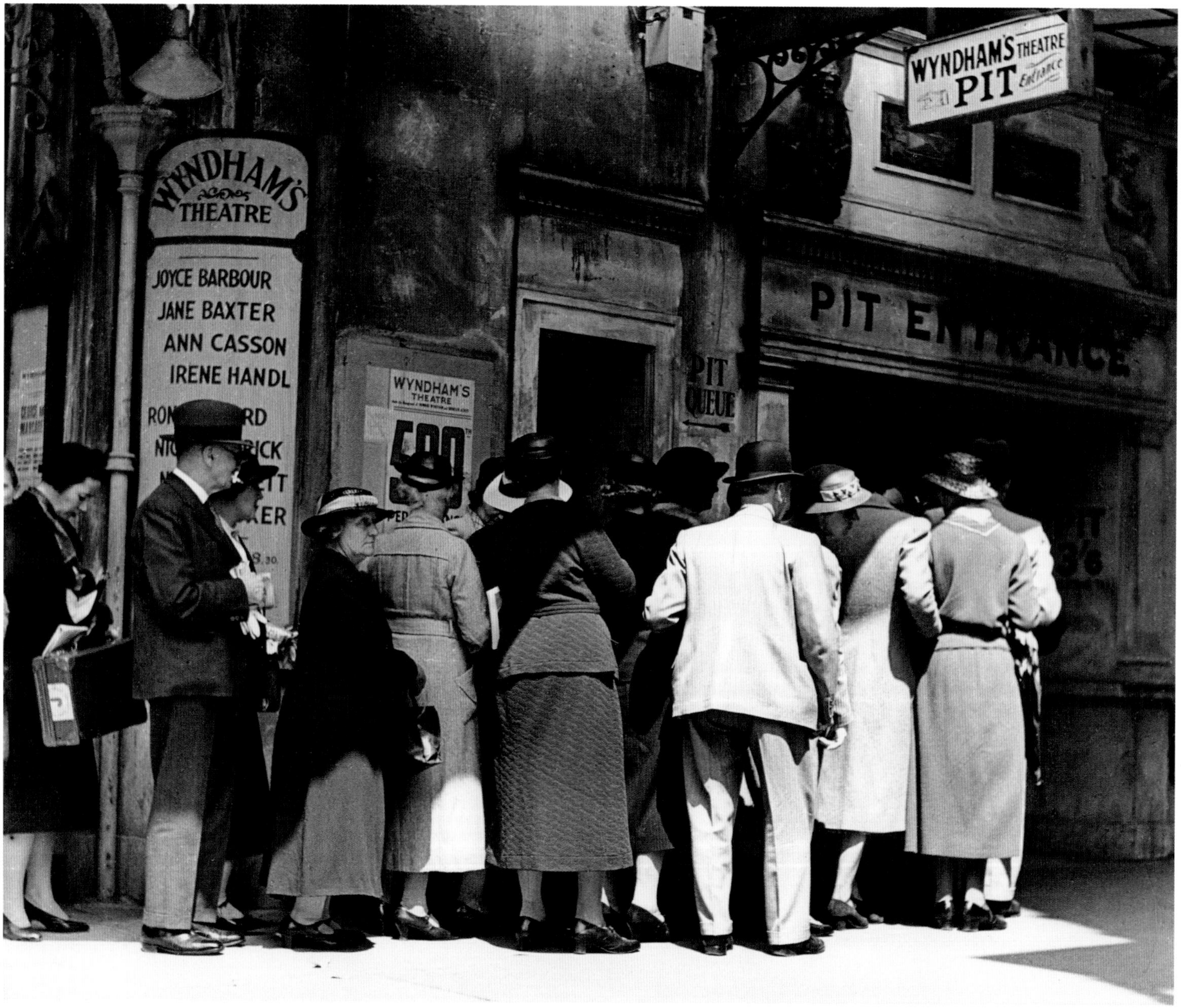
WYNDHAM'S THEATRE
JOYCE BARBOUR
JANE BAXTER
ANN CASSON
IRENE HANDL
WYNDHAM'S THEATRE
WYNDHAM'S THEATRE PIT Entrance
PIT QUEUE

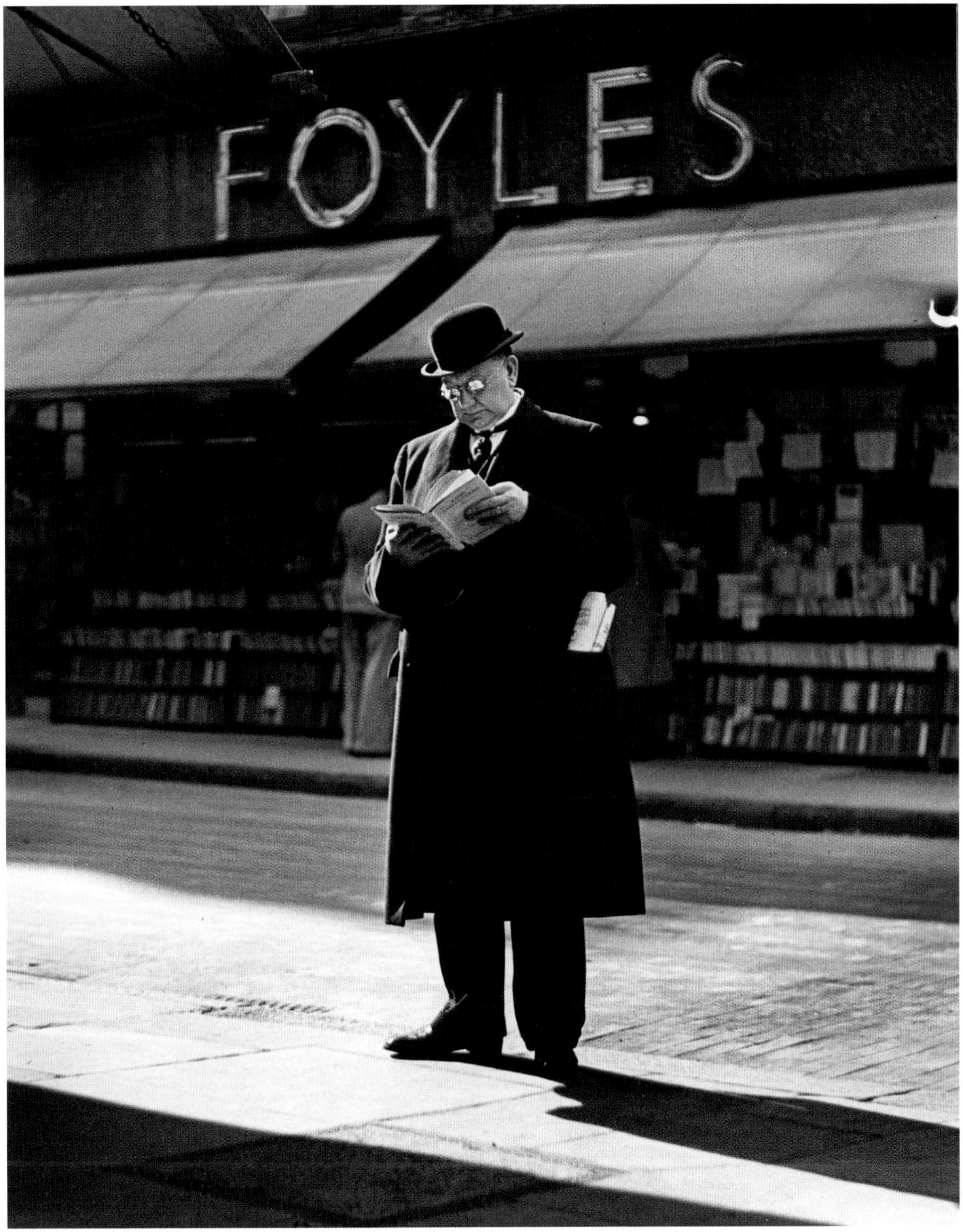
FOYLES

Dorothy Bohm
Paris

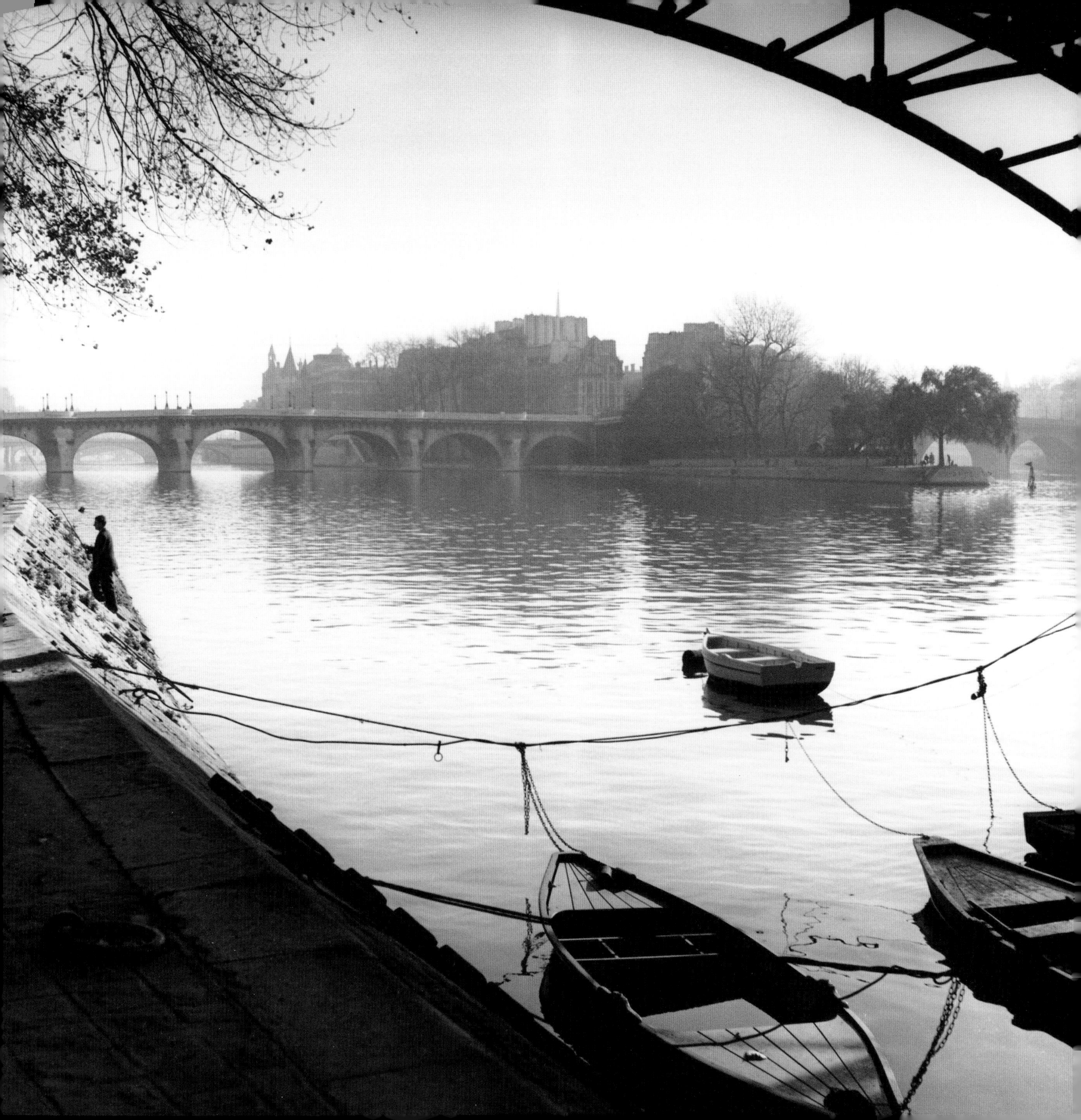

Dorothy Bohm and Paris

A Proustian community (and romance), revisited[1]

Michael Berkowitz

As an urbane European born in Königsberg in 1924, who travels widely and has spent much of her adult life in London, it is not surprising that Dorothy Bohm has a significant component of her portfolio – and a warm spot in her heart – devoted to Paris. For many Jews who experienced the trauma of dislocation and destruction of their former homes, and the murder of their remaining family members, the cities of New York, London and Paris emit an array of potent mythologies, something like a magnetic field. Dorothy grew up in Memel (Klaipeda), in the west of Lithuania, where her father was a textile magnate. Some ninety-five per cent of her fellow Litvaks did not survive the Holocaust. Dorothy's affinity for Paris is similar to that of several of her contemporaries who emerged as extraordinarily talented photographers, such as Izis (Israel Bidermanas), Gisèle Freund, Ferenc Berko, Robert Capa, Chim (David Seymour), Willy Ronis, and Dorothy's dear friend, André Kertész. All of them have been described as some variety of wanderer between worlds, with Paris serving as a beacon.

The selection of photographs in the current exhibition allows Dorothy to reflect back on an earlier, extensive show of her work, in both black and white and colour, *Un amour de Paris*, held at the Musée Carnavalet a decade ago, from September to December, 2005. Along with the tremendous honour of having a substantial collection of her photographs presented, with a handsome catalogue including scholarly essays, Dorothy was deeply touched by the public's demonstration of their appreciation for her understanding of their home. It is a point of pride for Dorothy that this was possibly the first catalogue of the Carnavalet to have a full English translation along with the French text.[2] (The most recent, spectacular exhibition of women photographers in Paris, *Qui a peur des femmes photographes?* has a catalogue exclusively in French.[3]) Large crowds appeared at the Carnavalet in the autumn and winter of 2005 and many individuals made a point of writing to Dorothy personally. Posters advertising the show were plastered all over the city, including the Metro stations. Among the many reasons why Dorothy regards Paris as one of the world's most sophisticated capitals is because for many years it stood nearly alone in featuring photography in its major art museums.

The Ben Uri presentation affords Dorothy an opportunity not only to exhibit a record of what she saw in Paris in the 1950s, but to share work that personally means a great deal to her: 'what I really wanted to photograph'. The first time she visited the city, in 1947, it was rather down-at-heel, suffering from the ravages of wartime. She believes that fundamental aspects of its character, and that of its people, revealed themselves nevertheless. On that trip, and into the next decade, it was not difficult to find those who were interested in art for art's sake – and who seemed largely oblivious to

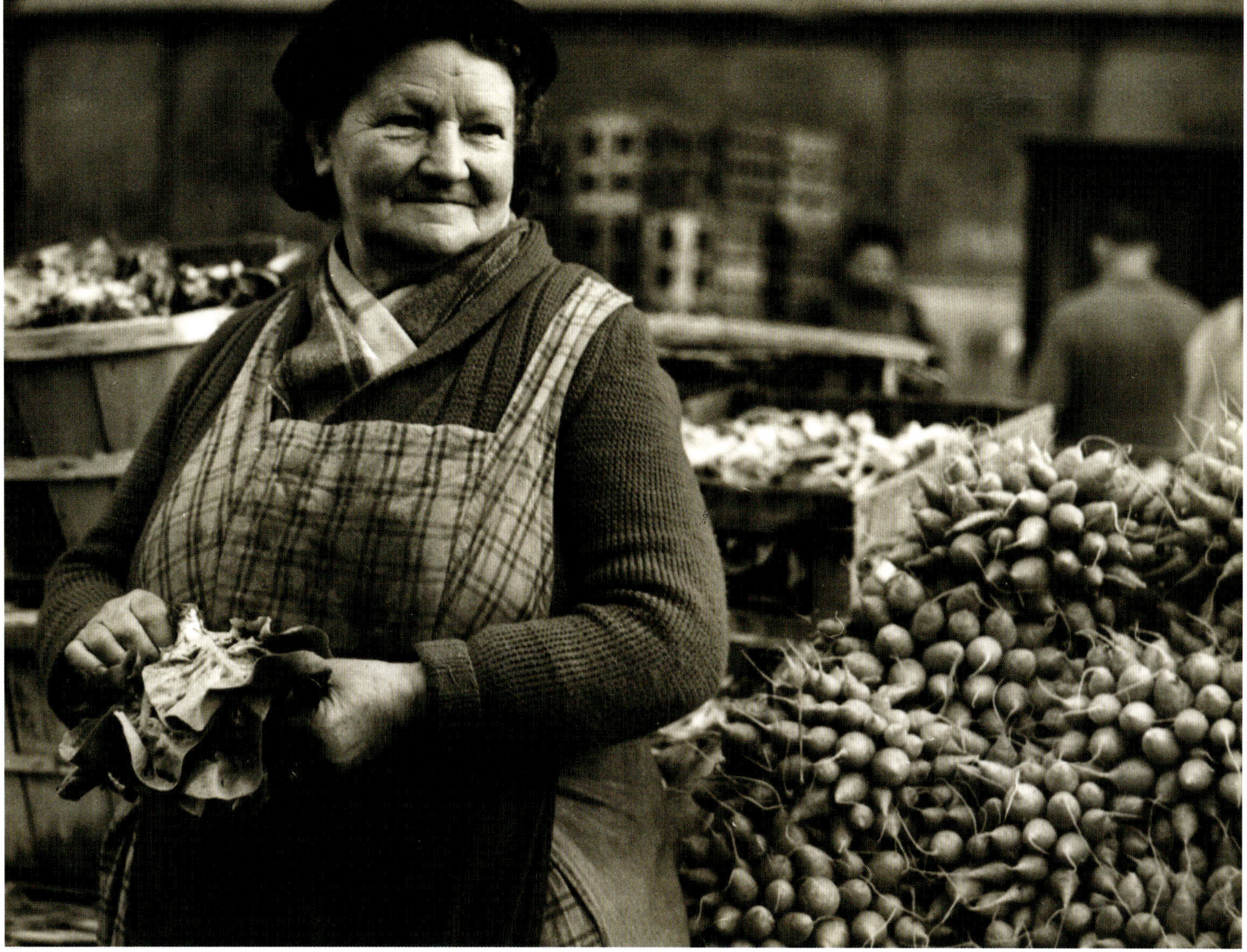

Les Halles, 1953

what had transpired beyond them. This is apparent in the work from 1950 of three men observing a painter in the Place du Tertre (p. 61). Another photo labelled simply *Paris, 1958*, a painter being watched by a young girl, is one of her favourites (p. 56). It was taken in the autumn by the Seine, a scene she feels is 'very Paris'.

While her photography in Paris was conducted in a sort of splendid isolation, with the unstinting support of her late husband, Louis, Dorothy also wishes to express her appreciation for the artist Avigdor Arikha, whose portrait was made on several occasions by Henri Cartier-Bresson (and vice versa).[4] Arikha befriended her and showed her around the city, introducing Dorothy to surroundings beyond tourist Paris, a real insider's view, with studied thought given to the routes of their excursions. She recalls that he asked her, once, to hand over her camera, and he then proceeded to photograph something 'quite ordinary' – perhaps a rubbish bin. She realised that there was something poetic about it, and that ordinary objects and apparently mundane scenes can, in a different manner to the *Neue Sachlichkeit* of Germany in the 1920s and early 1930s, take on an enlivened quality.

Although Dorothy does not see herself as being influenced by other photographers generally,[5] she no doubt shared the sentiment of André Kertész that 'The camera is my tool. Through it I give a reason to everything around me.'[6] Upon Arikha's death *The New York Times* wrote that his work 'captured both the haunting beauty and the looming menace of everyday things, a vision informed in no small part by his experience as a Holocaust survivor'.[7] Beginning his career as an abstract artist, Arikha turned to still lifes and portraits in the mid-1960s. It is little wonder that he evinced a tremendous interest in Dorothy's photographs. Perhaps they resonated for him as a transition from concern for the abstract to more concrete entities that he himself was beginning to work through. 'Unusually for a working artist, Mr Arikha also wrote extensively on art history' and curated a number of exhibitions.[8] With Arikha as her trusted companion, Bohm recalls that she spent a year in Paris 'looking with the camera and loving it'.

Bohm loved Paris as a fixed place but, even more, her feelings were inextricable from the people who helped inspire and nurture her impressions – including Marie Nordlinger (1886–1970). Dorothy knew Nordlinger from her early years in Manchester, in the 1940s. Dorothy's father-in-law was acquainted with Nordlinger's brother, who also headed a textile firm, which provided the entrée for Louis and Dorothy into the sumptuous Manchester home Marie shared with her brother.[9] Marie Nordlinger is now best remembered as a collaborator of Marcel Proust, one who was especially important in assisting Proust in his translations and understanding of John Ruskin,[10] the most important writer on art in Victorian England, whose interests, opinions and talents ranged widely. (Dorothy, of course, was too young to have known Proust, as he died in 1922, but she had long been familiar with Proust's *À la recherche du temps perdu*.) In addition, her reverence for, and acknowledgement of the importance of Proust in seeing Paris with great self-consciousness, was transmitted to her through her fellow photographer, Brassaï, who himself wrote about Proust and photography.[11] Yet it is likely that Nordlinger also had a strong sense of Ruskin's little-mentioned high regard for photography – unusual for his time – and the extent to which photography influenced his own art and thought about aesthetics. Rather than demeaning photography, as the otherwise brilliant Susan Sontag asserts,[12] Proust, as Seth Wolitz and Mary Bergstein have argued, had contradictory yet complex ideas about photography's importance. He appreciated finely executed photographic reproductions of paintings and architecture, writing to Nordlinger in 1905: 'In my intentionally *naked* room, there is only one reproduction of a work of art: an excellent photograph of Whistler's *Carlyle*, in a serpentine overcoat like the dress in the portrait of his mother. The more I think about the theories of Ruskin and Whistler, the more I believe they are not irreconcilable.'[13] In the early 1950s, the pioneering historian of photography, Helmut Gernsheim – another refugee from Hitler's Germany – attempted to call attention to the significance of Ruskin's photography, but few were willing to listen.[14] 'Comparing his own view of Venice with a painting by Canaletto made from the same standpoint, Ruskin declared himself decidedly in favour of the daguerreotype "in which every figure, crack and stain is given on the scale of an inch to Canaletto's three feet."'[15] As opposed to Whistler's sartorial *Carlyle* (at the Kelvingrove Art Gallery and Museum, Glasgow), however, none of Dorothy's portraits from Paris in the 1950s have names attached, as all are of common people, and the most 'high-class' image may be that of a well-coiffed poodle.

Ruskin's concern for detail, and the constructedness of the built environment, shines through several of Dorothy's Paris photographs. Her view of *The Seine, Quai du Louvre and Pont-Neuf*, 1955 (p. 68) is elegant and scientific – geometric, natural and beautiful.

Some of her photographs draw in and hold the viewer. Her photograph *Antique Shop, Rue La Boétie*, 1956 (p. 67), is not an inanimate window display, but features the attractive, poised proprietress imploring Dorothy, it seems, to take the picture, but also to consider that this is her livelihood – the photographer might buy something, too. Dorothy's *Goat Carriage, Tuileries Gardens*, 1953 (p. 65) captures the goat and includes children on the park bench, one of whom is sleepy from the day out. In *Twins, Villa des Tulipes, 18th arrondissement, near the Marché aux Puces*, 1953, (p. 64) she also allows us a view of a set of twins, with matching headscarves, peering into a pram and tending to its occupant – possibly their younger sibling or maybe a doll. There is nothing alive around them, though. They are on an empty, narrow brick street with hard, flat surfaces surrounding them. Brilliantly composed, the only curves and circles are found in the children and the pram, all else is lines and sharp angles.

There is no main motif in Dorothy's Paris of the 1950s. We see the Seine, buildings, trees, animals and people – some matters are commercial, while others are indifferent to the realm of the market. There is a calm quality to all of these, as Bohm was not in a hurry to get a shot of a famous person, and she was not trying to photograph something unusual that could be sold to the press. These photographs show not only her Paris, but a Paris that has been, and will remain, of interest to countless others, because it speaks to them of their own sense of, and profound love for, the city of light.

Rue Lepic, Montmartre, 1955 (detail)

[1] The title is an affectionate appropriation from Seth Wolitz, *The Proustian Community* (New York: New York University Press, 1971). Wolitz, in his pathbreaking work, was the first scholar to note the importance of photography in the work and life of Marcel Proust.

[2] Mark Haworth-Booth *et al.*, *Un amour de Paris: photographs by / photographies de Dorothy Bohm* (Paris: Paris musées, 2005).

[3] *Qui a peur des femmes photographes? 1839–1945* (Paris: Musée d'Orsay, 2015).

[4] See Dan Hofstadter, ed., *Temperaments: Artists Facing Their Work* (New York: Knopf, 1992), which includes memoirs of Cartier-Bresson and Arikha.

[5] Françoise Reynaud, 'L'aventure d'une vie dans la photographie/A life in photography', in *Un amour de Paris*, p. 31, note 19.

[6] Quote in Susan Sontag, *On Photography* (London: Penguin, 1979), p. 207.

[7] Margalit Fox, 'Avigdor Arikha, Artist of the Everyday, Is Dead at 81', *New York Times* (1 May 2010), p. 8.

[8] Ibid.

[9] Lynne Woolfson, 'Un long chemin vers Paris/The Long Road to Paris', in *Un amour de Paris*, p. 23.

[10] See Pat F. Prestwich, *The Translation of Memories: Recollections of the Young Proust* (London: Peter Owen, 1999).

[11] Brassaï, *Marcel Proust sous l'emprise de la Photographie* (Paris: Gallimard, 1997).

[12] Sontag, *On Photography*, p. 164.

[13] Mary Bergstein, *In Looking Back One Learns to See: Proust and Photography* (Amsterdam and New York: Rodopi, 2014), p. 85, note 176; see Wolitz, pp. 138–40.

[14] See Michael Berkowitz, *Jews and Photography in Britain* (Austin: University of Texas Press, 2015), p. 218.

[15] Helmut Gernsheim, *Creative Photography: Aesthetic Trends 1839–1960* (New York: Bonanza Books, 1962), p. 25, quoting John Ruskin, *The Seven Lamps of Architecture* (1849).

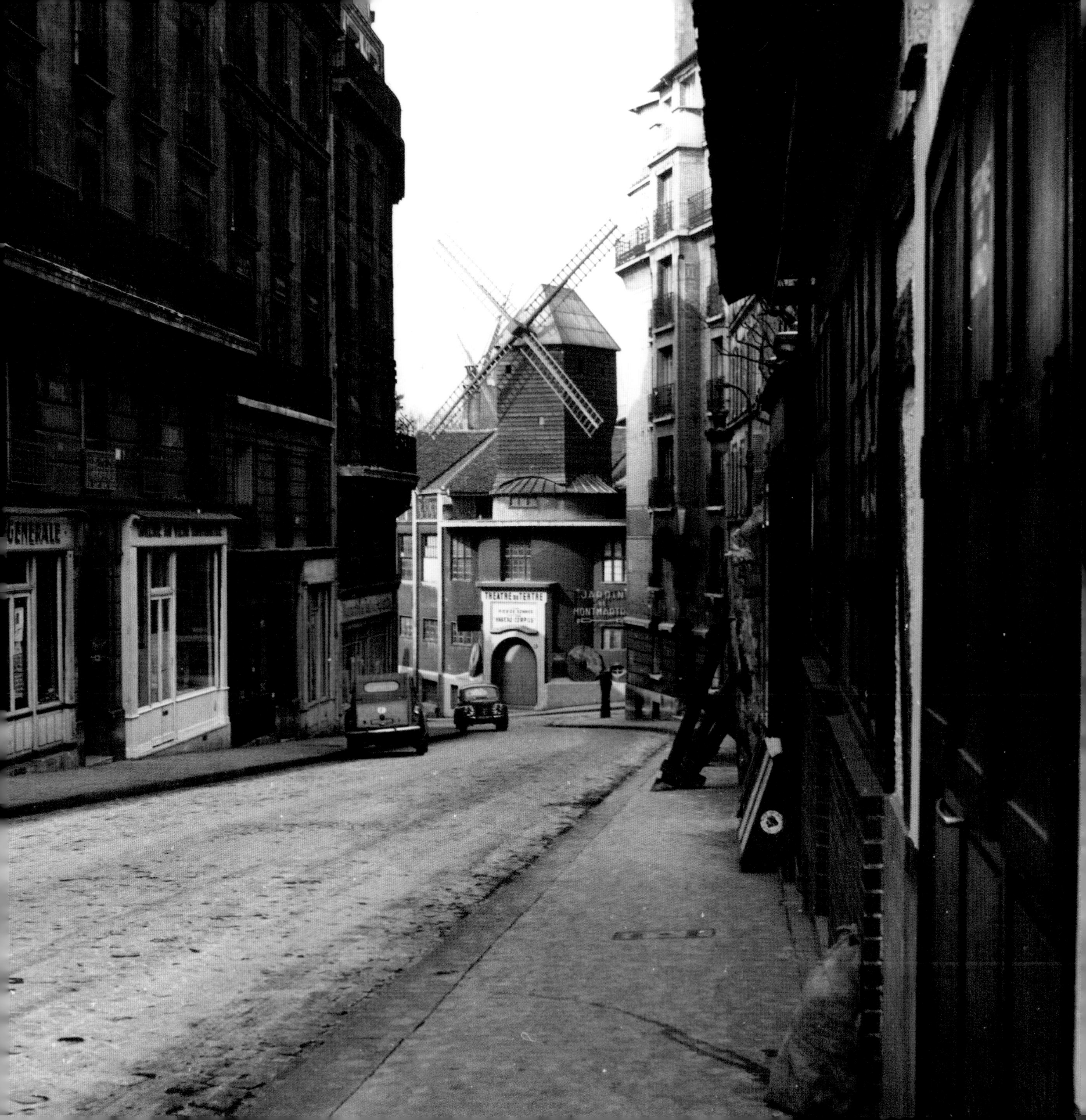
GENERALE
THEATRE DU TERTRE
JARDIN

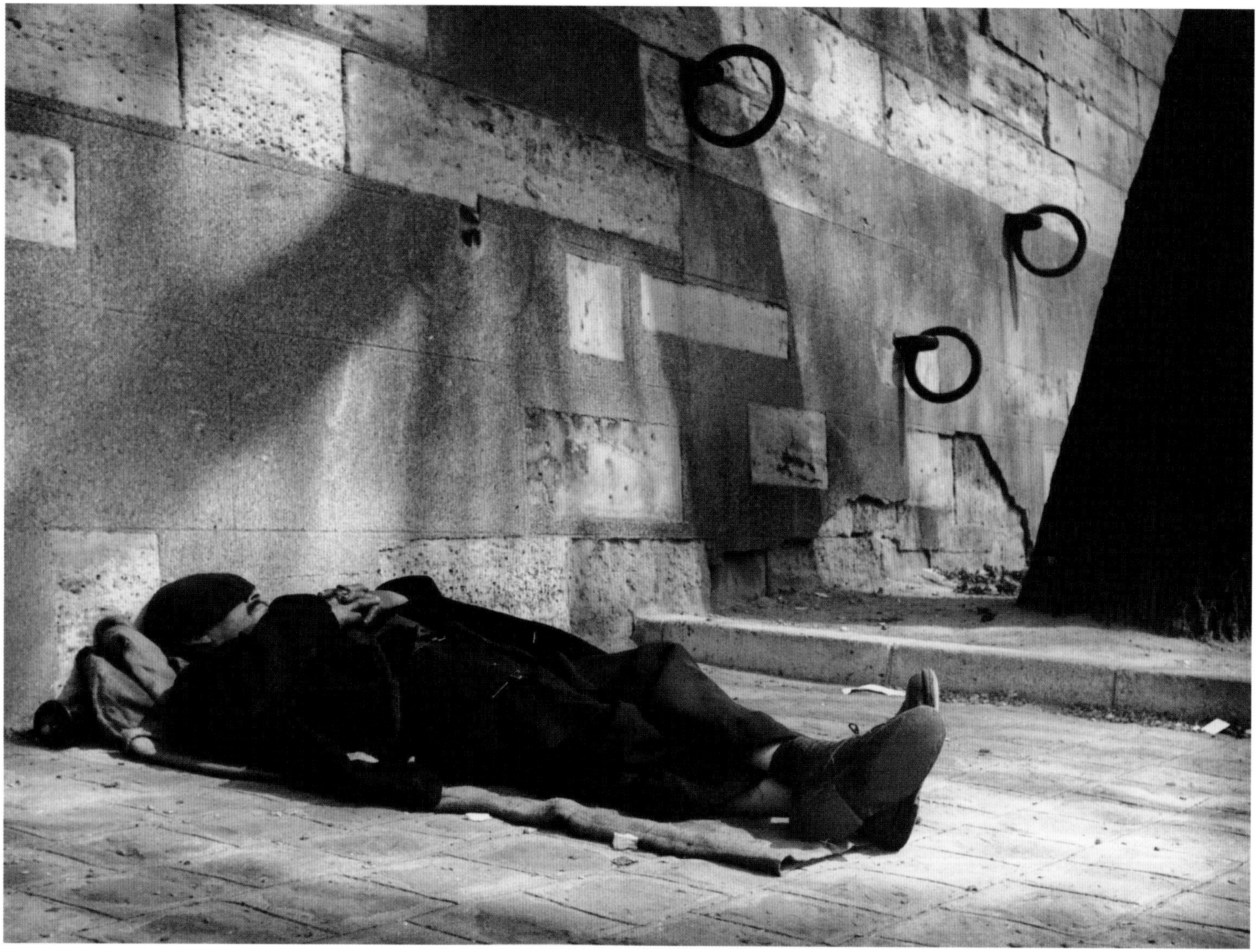

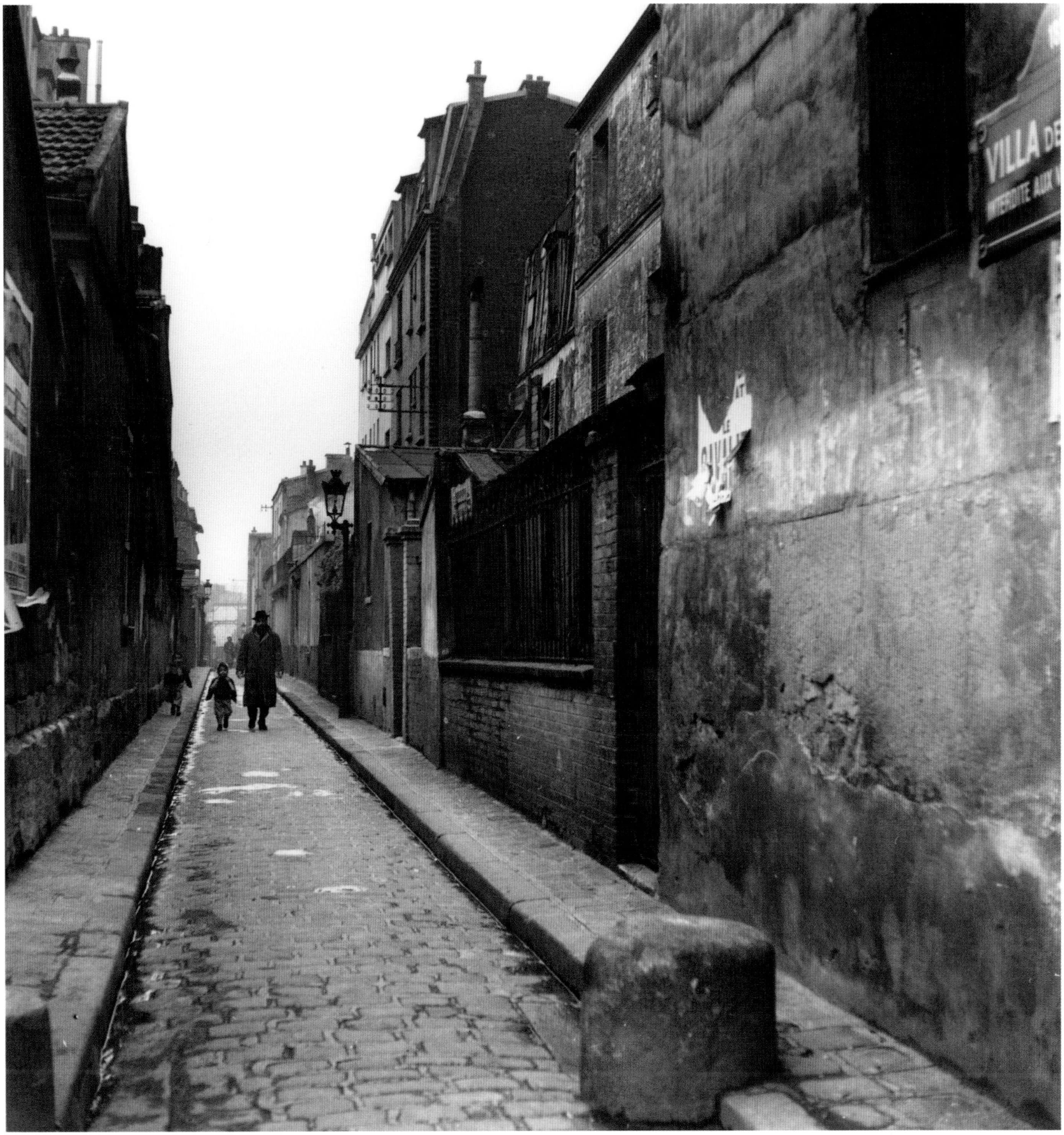
VILLA DE

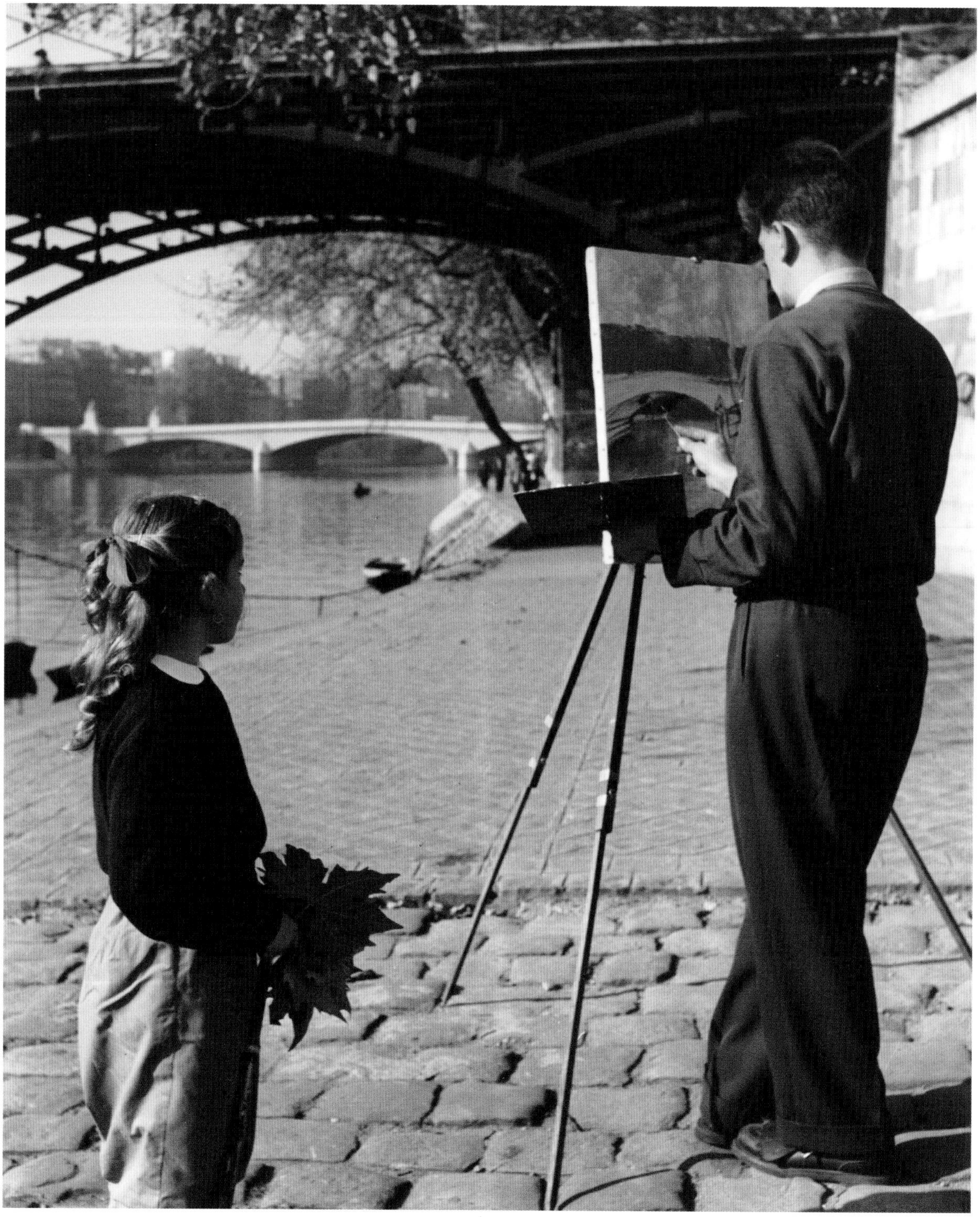

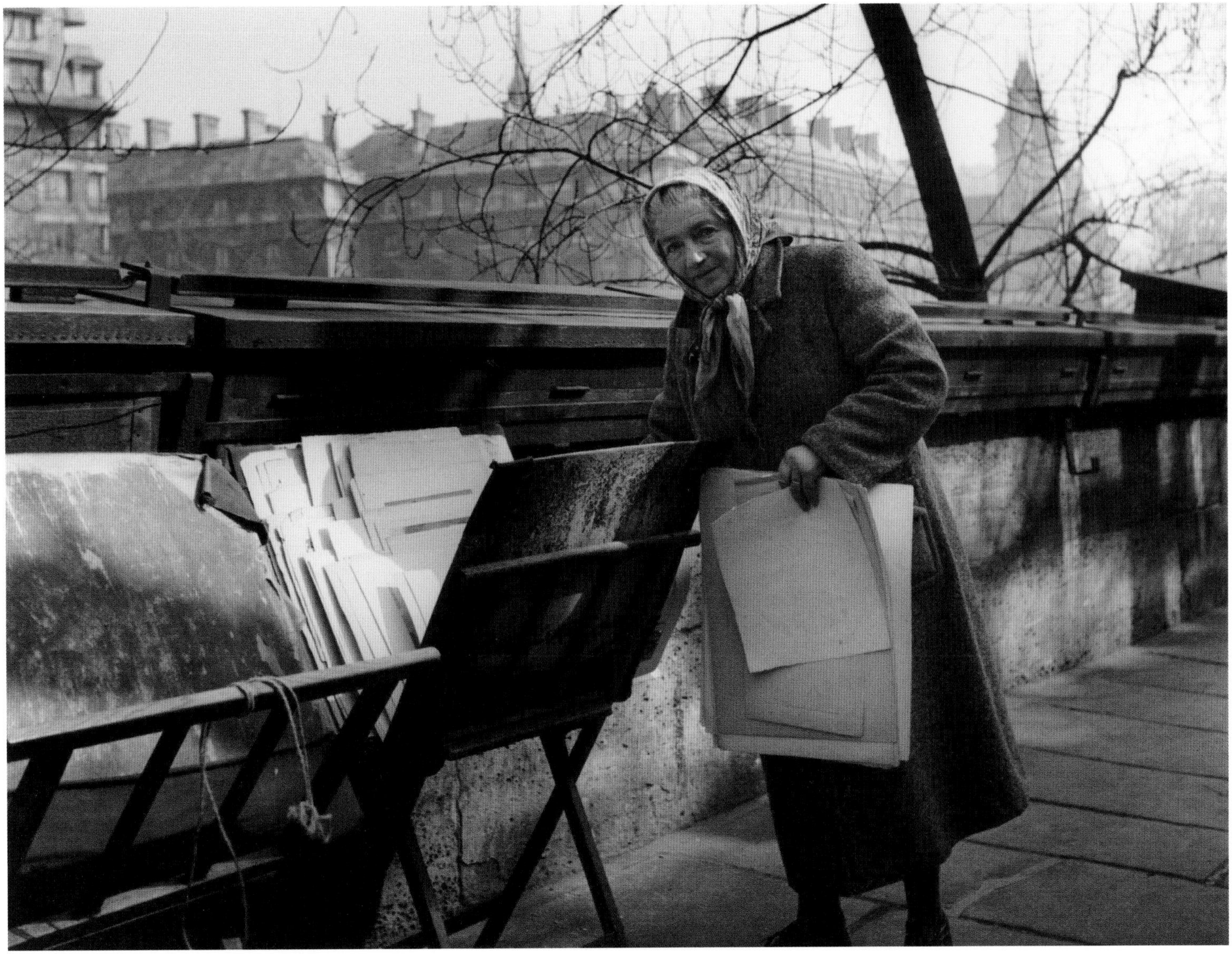

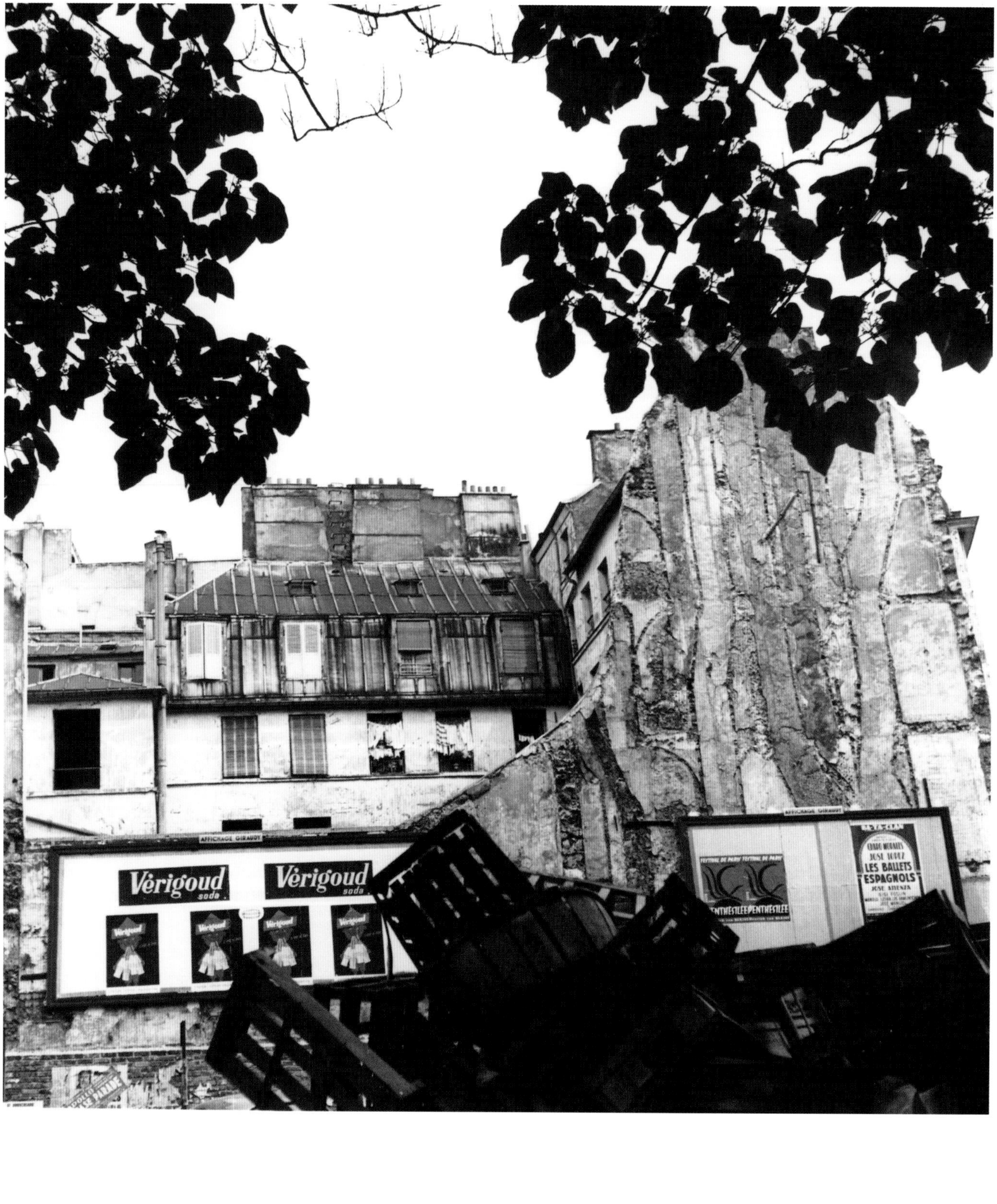
AFFICHAGE GIRAUDY
Vérigoud
soda
Vérigoud
soda
PENTHESILEE PENTHESILEE
LES BALLETS
ESPAGNOLS

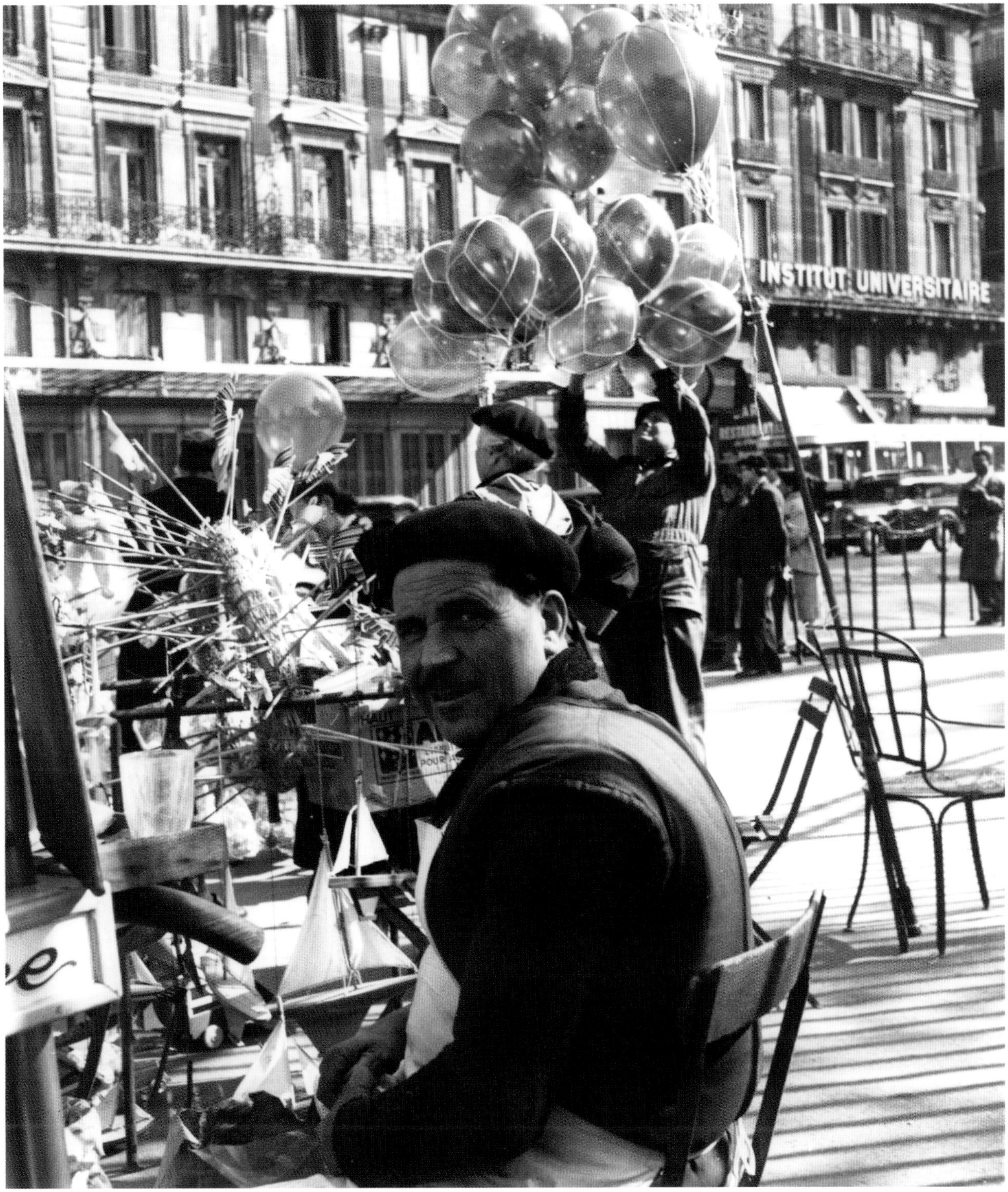
INSTITUT UNIVERSITAIRE

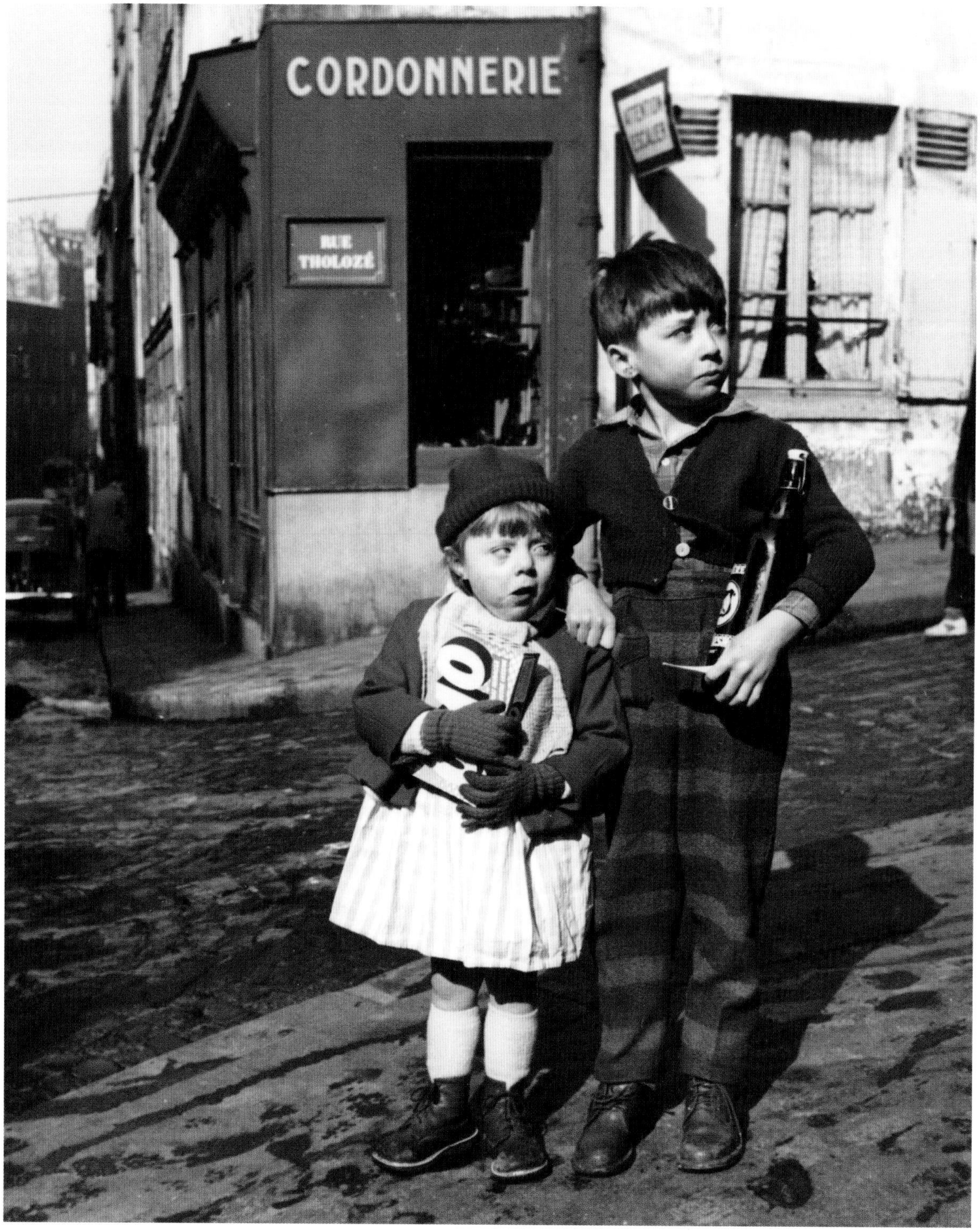
CORDONNERIE
RUE THOLOZÉ

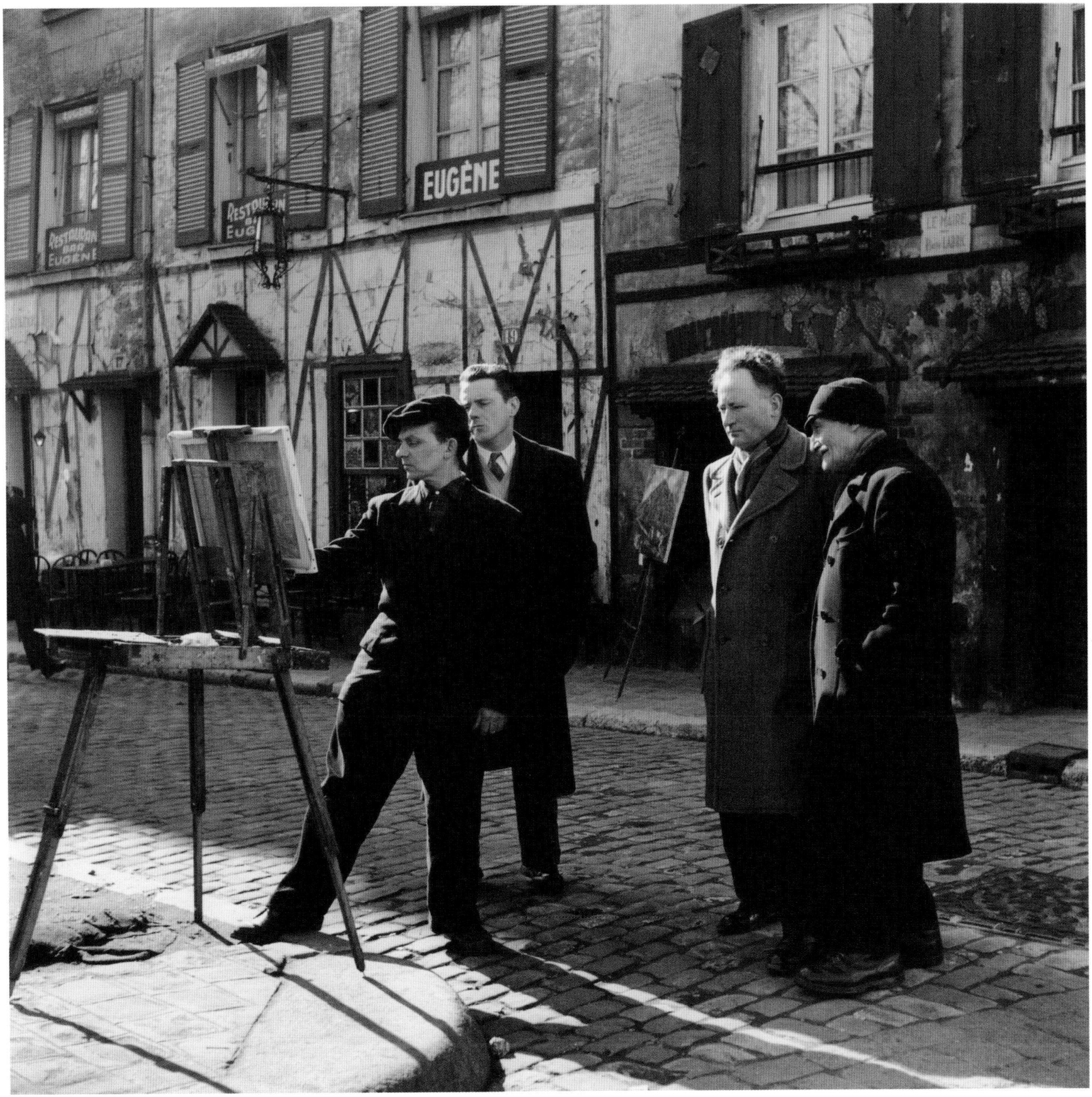
EUGÈNE

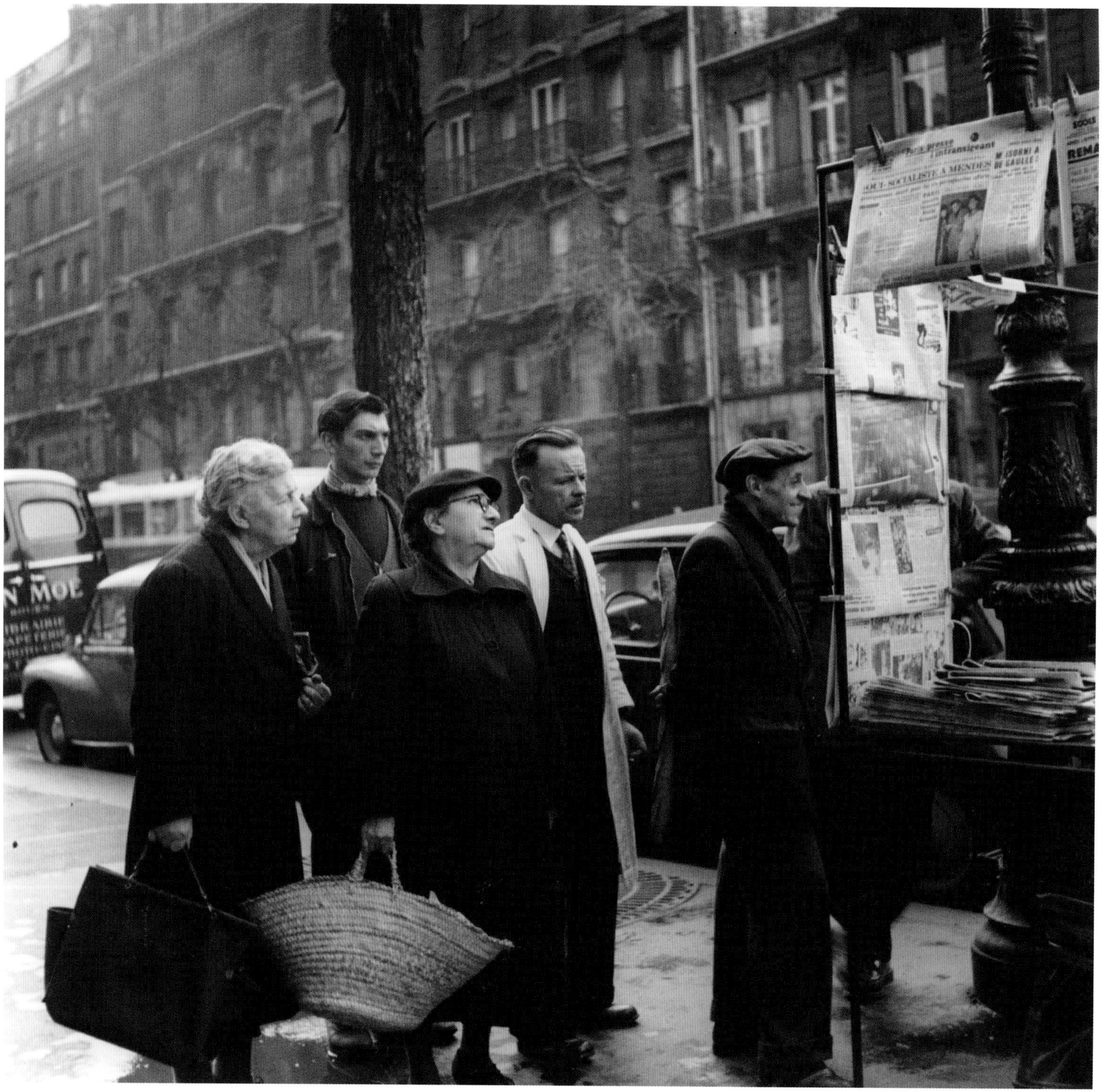

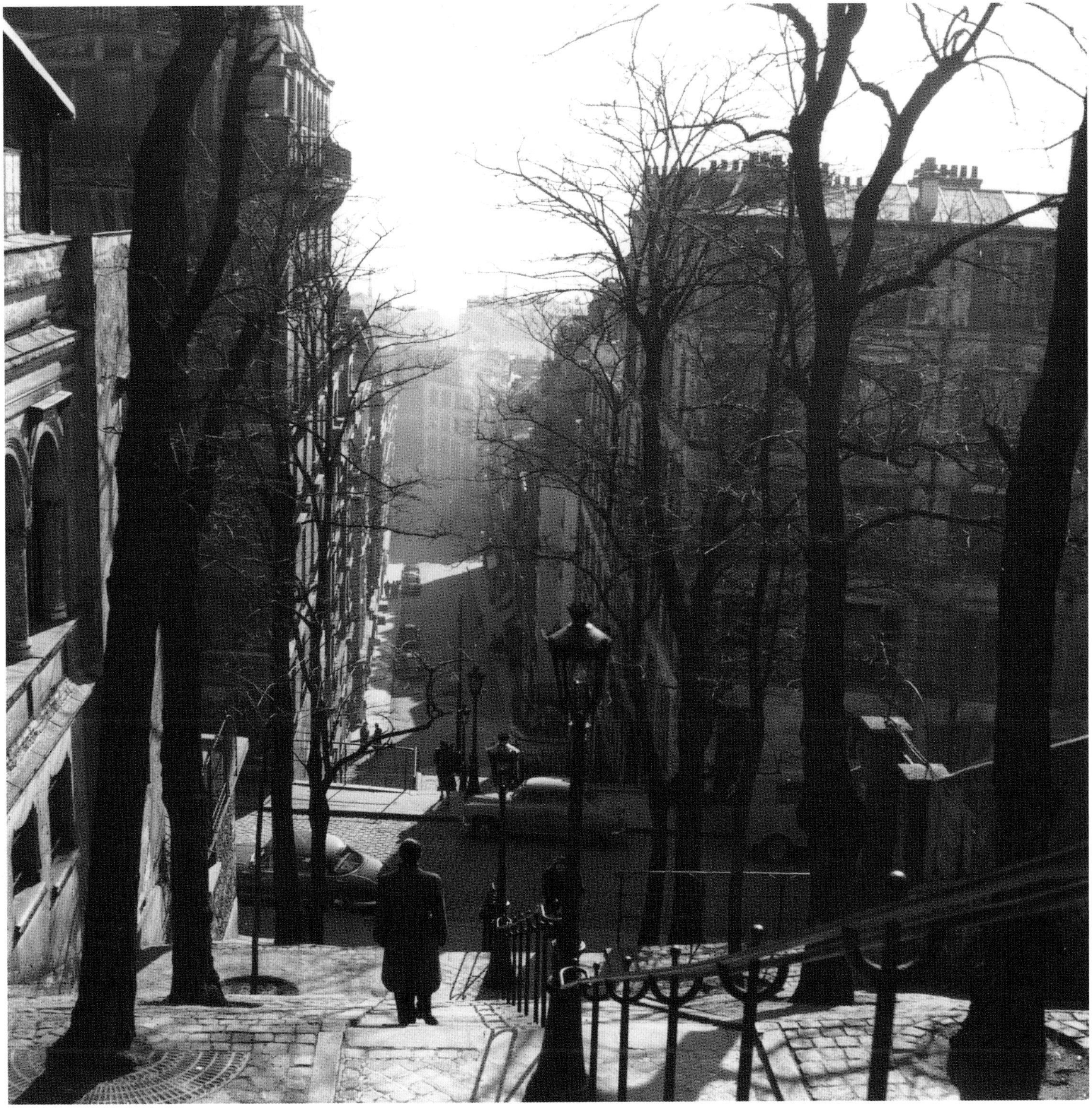

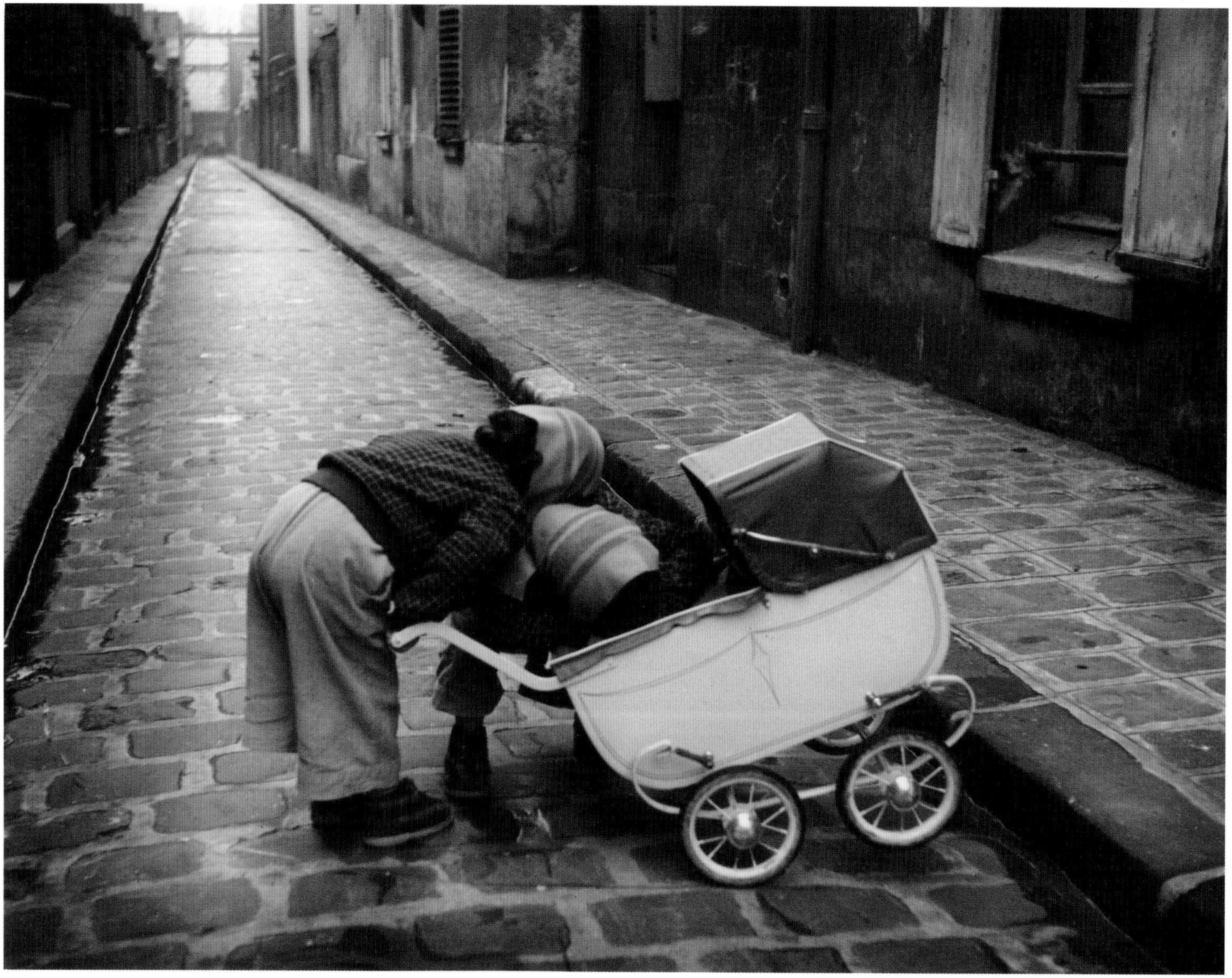

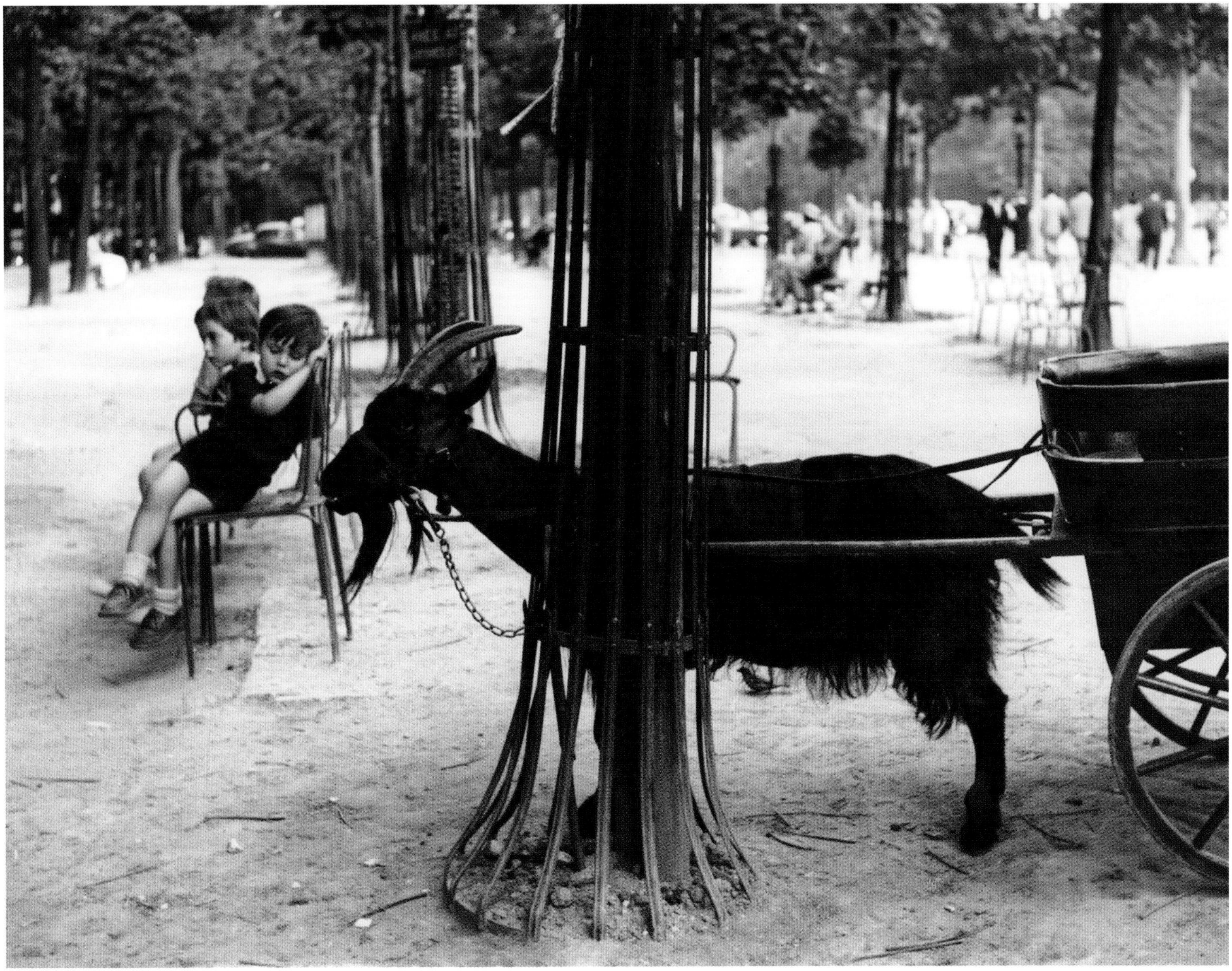

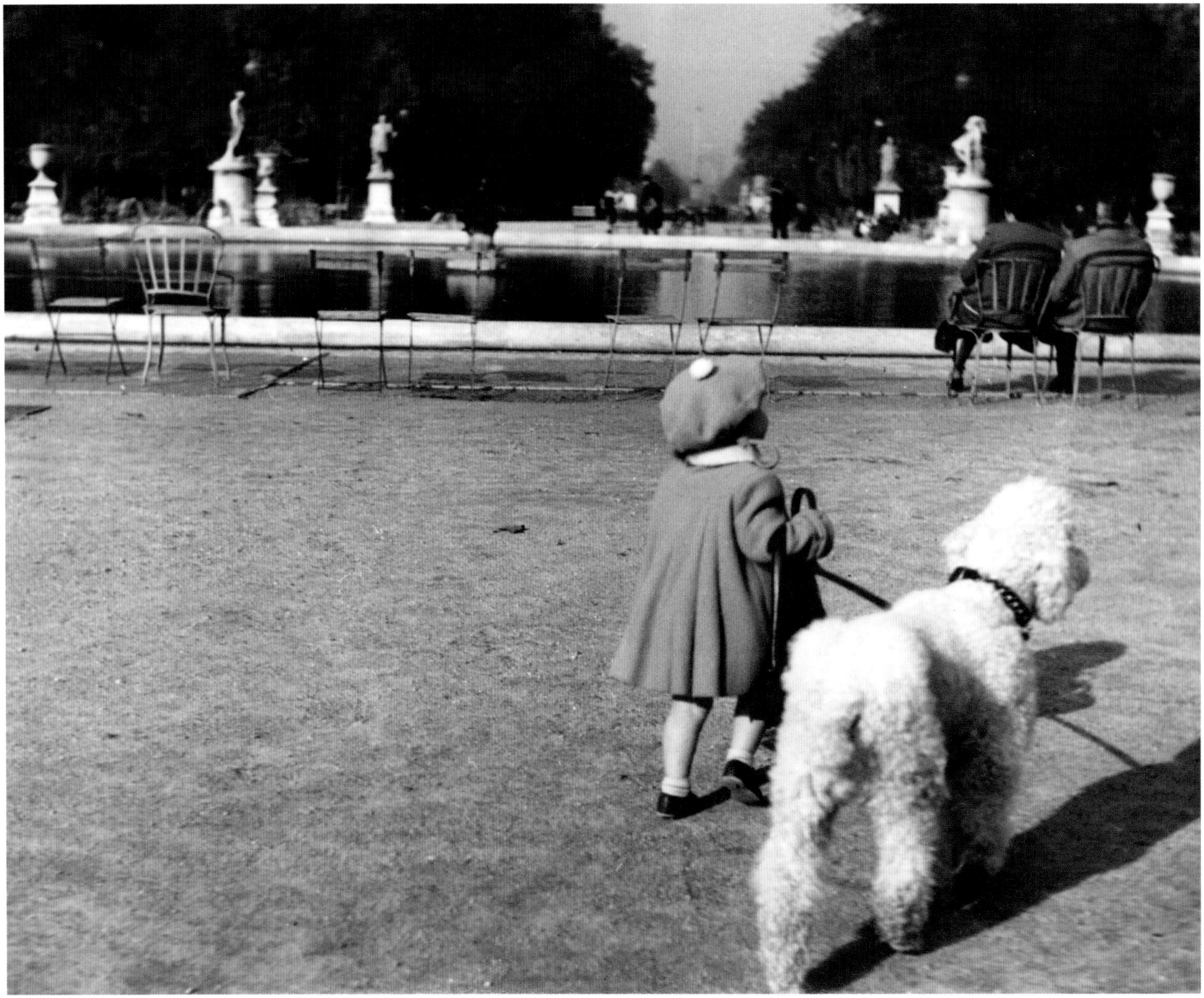

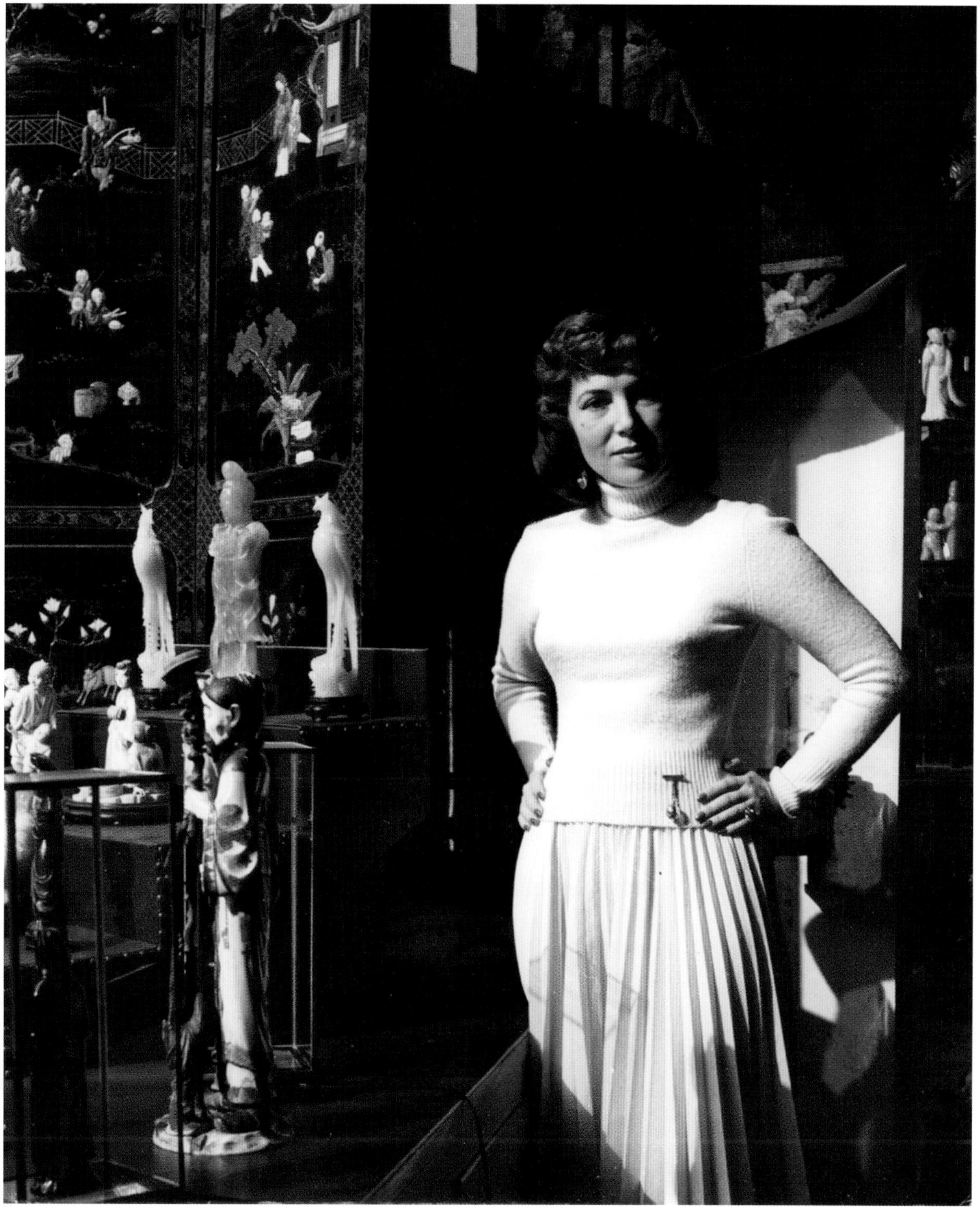

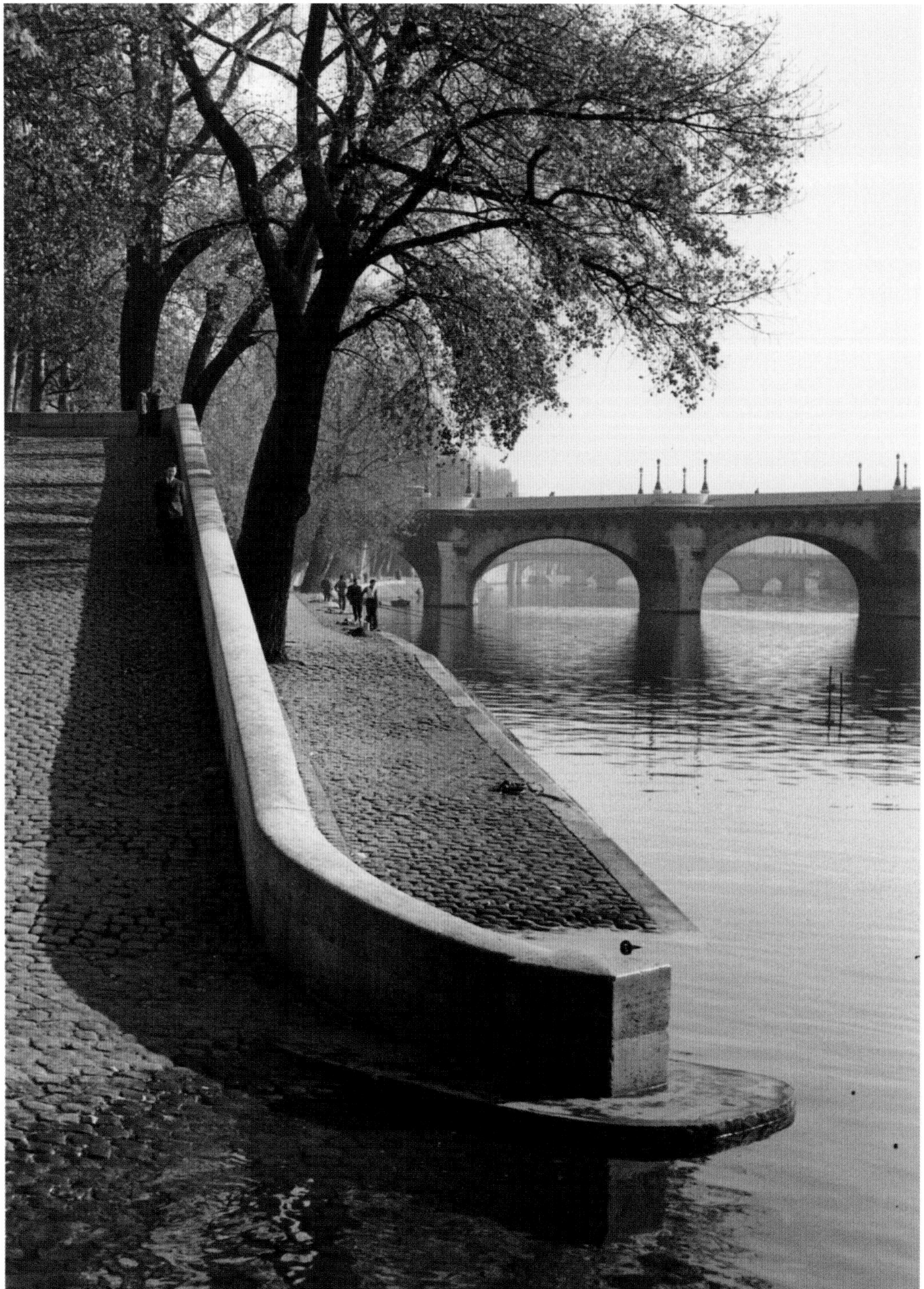

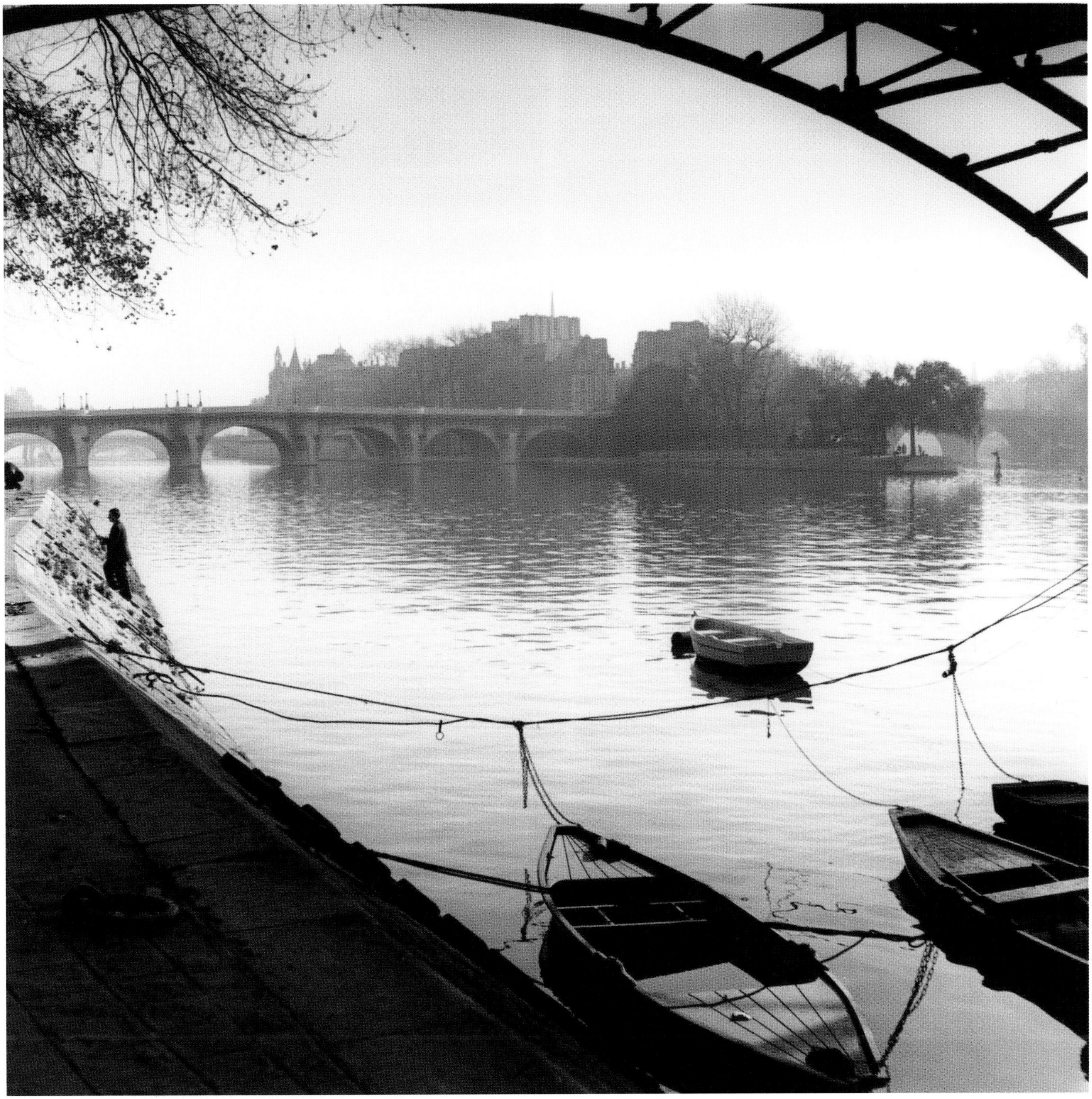

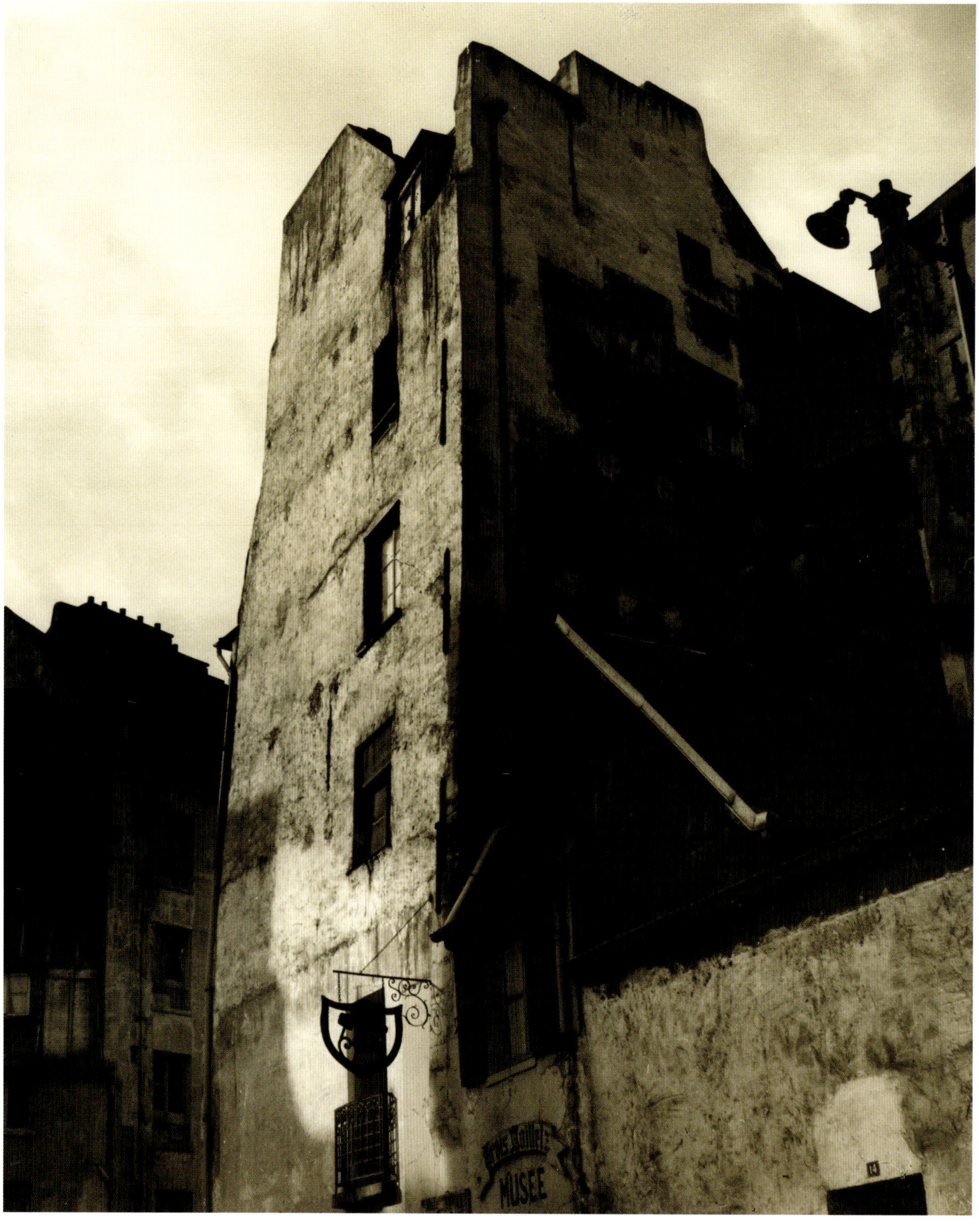
MUSEE

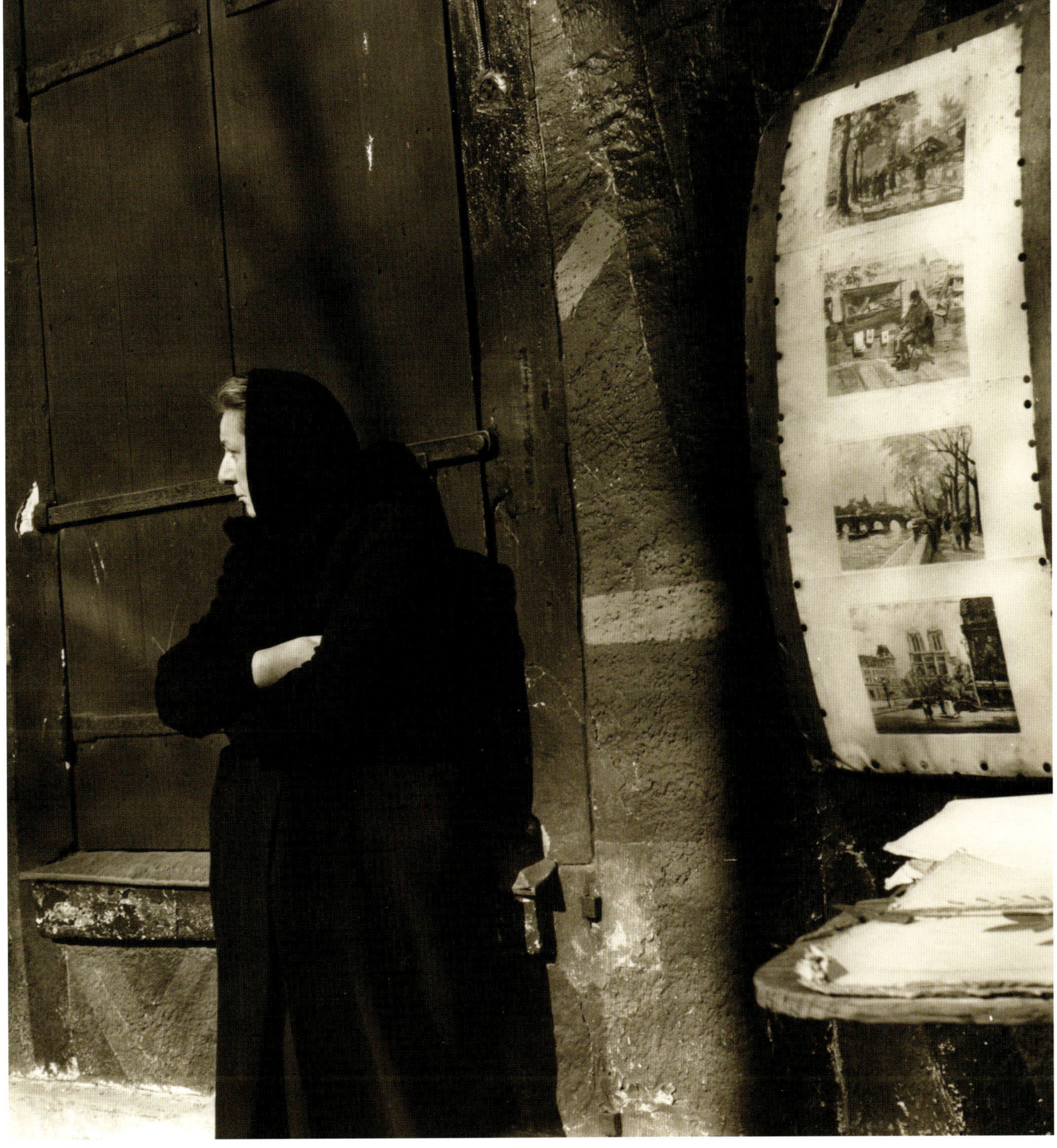

Neil Libbert
New York

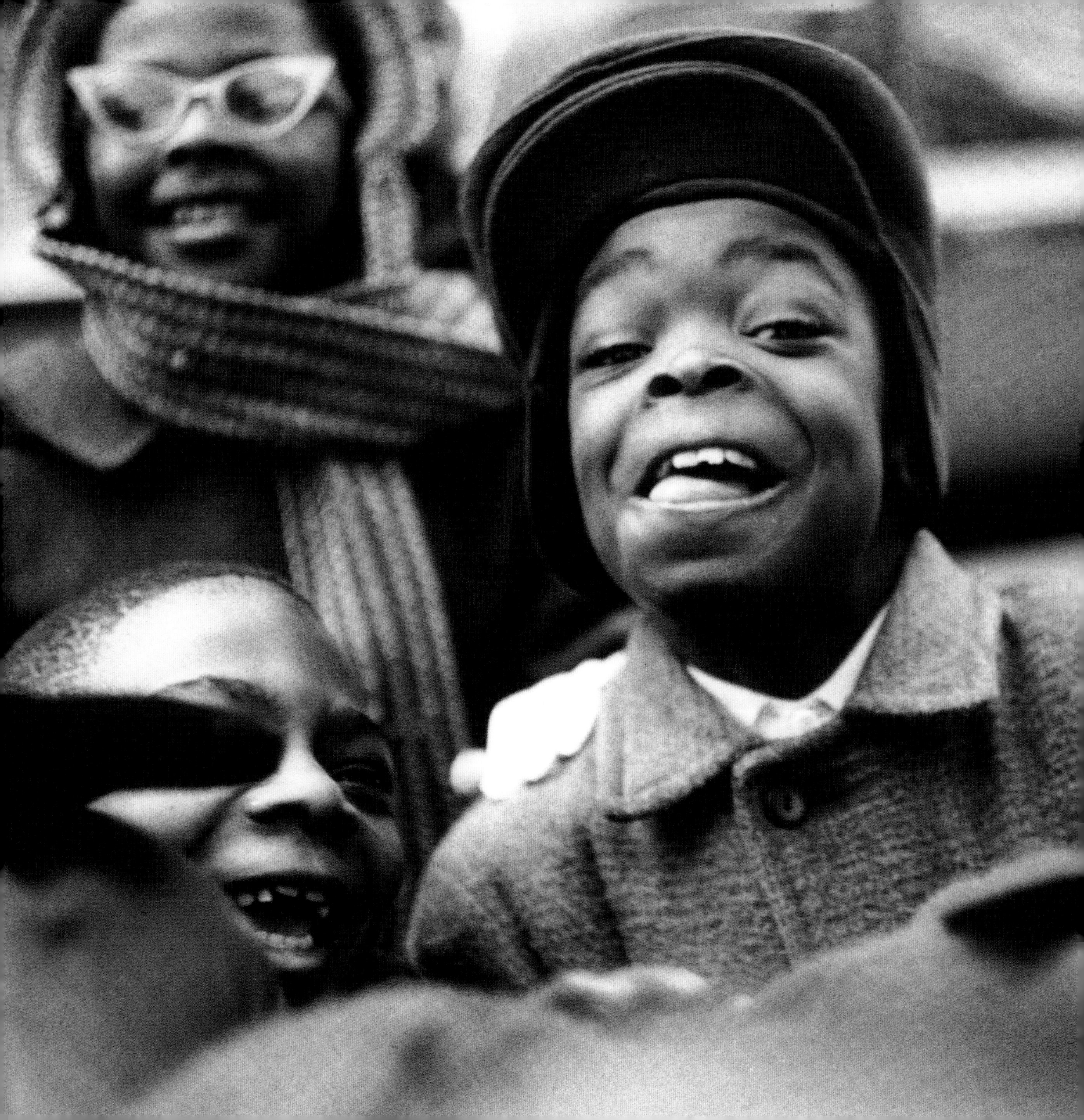

Neil Libbert
In conversation with Jessica Feather

Neil is well known for his reluctance to give interviews, but we have known one another for almost forty years so he agrees to a conversation with me. We meet at my flat. On many occasions, Neil's responses to my questions are a little reticent; he is not comfortable talking about himself or his works. He is most at ease when telling a story relating to the circumstances of a photograph, and it occurs to me afterwards that this is an important element of his pictures. They tell stories. They are about the people and relationships depicted in them.

It is worth emphasising that Neil is self-taught, with many of his first photographs being taken on the streets of Salford, Manchester during a period in which he was working at his father's factory. Apart from a time when he was salaried to the *Manchester Guardian*, Neil has largely remained freelance, and many of his works are not commissioned pieces. This approach is appropriate to Neil's fiercely independent vision. He is still a working photographer taking pictures both with a view to submitting them to newspapers but also for sheer pleasure. He is rarely without his camera in hand.

The following is an edited account of our conversation. We begin by talking in general terms about his photography.

Jessica Feather: I know you don't like giving interviews, why do you think that is?

Neil Libbert: The photographs should speak for themselves, and hopefully people like the pictures. I wouldn't know what to say if I had to talk about the pictures.

JF: Perhaps your primary medium isn't words, it's your pictures?

NL: I think that's right.

JF: Can we talk a little about how you think of yourself as a photographer? You've told me in the past that you are surprised by the many photography exhibitions on show now, and the way photographers are now considered to be artists. Do you think of yourself as a documentary photographer then, and not an artist?

NL: Yes.

JF: And presumably one more comfortable in black and white? You've quoted Cartier-Bresson at me in the past; and there are certainly strong influences to be seen in your work.

NL: Yes, I have to work in colour for the newspapers now, but I am much more at home with black and white.

JF: So, we are here to talk about your New York photographs. You first went to America in 1960, was that a work assignment?

NL: It was to accompany a journalist called William J. Weatherby, or Bill. He was on the paper [*Manchester Guardian*] as a writer, he eventually became a correspondent in New York, but at that time he was still living in London. I was there for a few months. I did some stories with Bill and then did my own thing. I went round on a Greyhound bus, that sort of thing. That was the first time. Then I went back quite a lot in the 1960s.

JF: What were your impressions of New York? You were a young man; it was probably your first time out of Europe. Was it glamorous?

NL: Yes, I suppose so. New World I suppose. New York was very exciting. It was a good city.

JF: But it was also a period of social unrest for the city. Were you aware of that?

NL: Harlem probably wasn't the safest place to be wandering around with a camera, and there were a lot of bricks being thrown around, but I had no problems.

JF: Where did you stay?

NL: Lots of odd places ... including the Chelsea Hotel. It was pretty notorious; extraordinary hotel, extraordinary people. Arthur Miller stayed there. The guy that owned it, Stanley Bard, liked me. Its lobby was full of Larry Rivers paintings.

JF: So some of these pictures in the Ben Uri show were part of this assignment, some weren't?

NL: Most of these pictures were not assigned. I took them when I was wandering around New York on my own. The commissioned pictures were mainly portraits ... people such as Carson McCullers [the American writer], who was pretty well known. Bill interviewed the people, and I did the pictures.

JF: So pictures like the child holding the gun [pp. 84] had nothing to do with the newspaper work?

NL: Yes. That was taken wandering the streets of Harlem on my own. It had nothing to do with the newspaper, although some of them were later illustrated in the newspaper.

JF: It is a really striking image. Was that taken during the 1964 race riot?

NL: Yes. I thought the fact that the boy was holding a replica gun was really interesting.

JF: It's not an obviously violent image though. The potential for violence is beautifully understated. You seem to be interested in the relationship between the policeman and the small child.

NL: I think that's right.

JF: Were people aware of you taking their photograph as you walked around?

NL: No, I don't think so.

JF: Other photographs you took in New York have become quite well known now. I'm thinking of your picture of the ice rink [p. 93], or the clock at Grand Central Station [p. 80]. Can you tell me a bit about these images?

NL: I can't really remember a lot about taking them.

JF: Perhaps you liked the composition? These are quite powerful.

NL: Yes, I suppose. [Talking about Grand Central Station] Look at the light coming down there, and the shadows, it's quite nice.

JF: There is a similarly interesting composition in the picture of the men with their legs crossed [p. 87]. Can you tell me about that?

NL: I went into the United Nations Building. I think that was taken from one of the translation booths. It struck me as rather fun, the way they were sitting.

JF: Many of your photos have people in them, that is something that unites them.

NL: Yes, I think that's true.

Neil is tired of being asked questions about his work. I make him a cup of tea and we talk about the exhibitions we are planning to visit.

3 April 2016

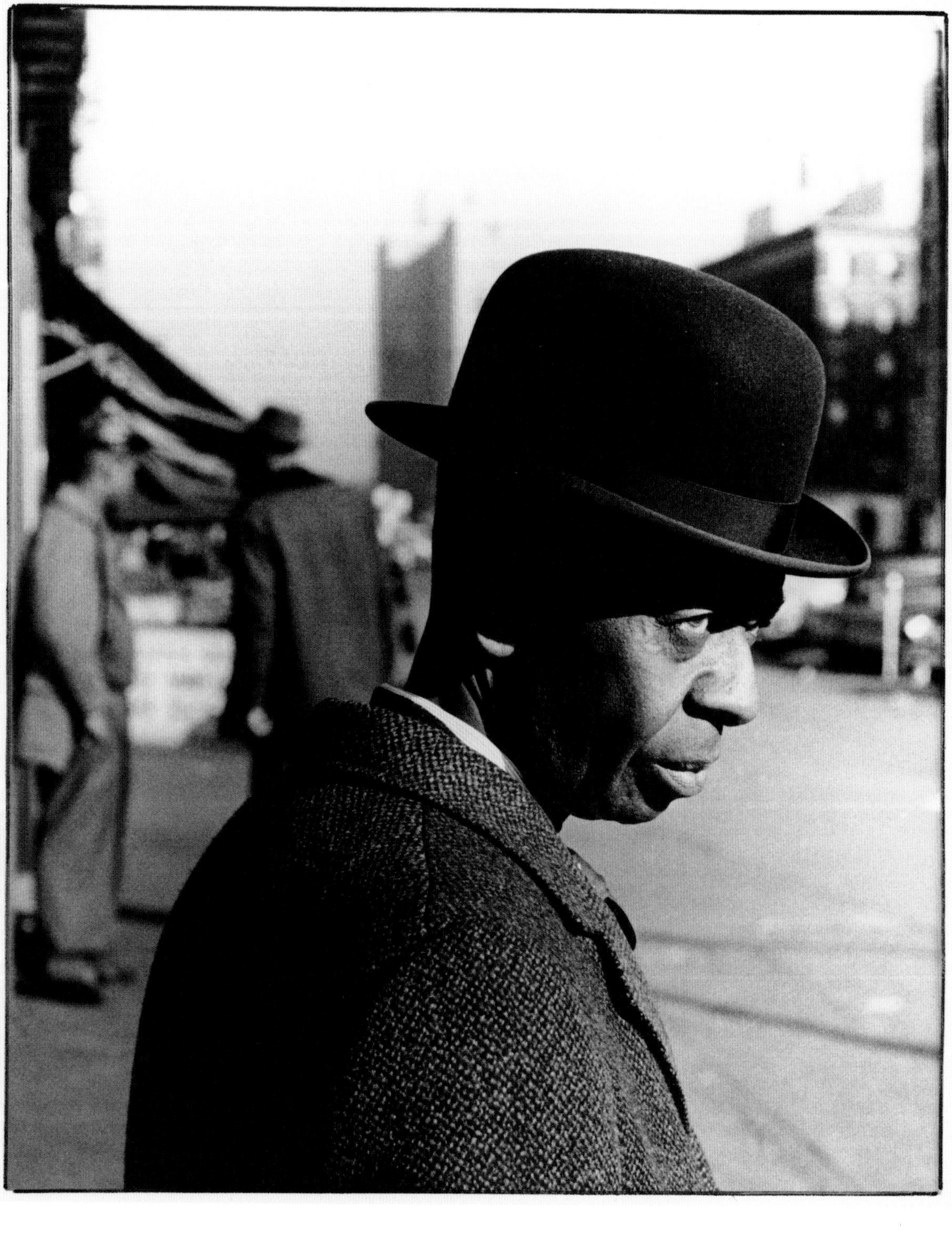

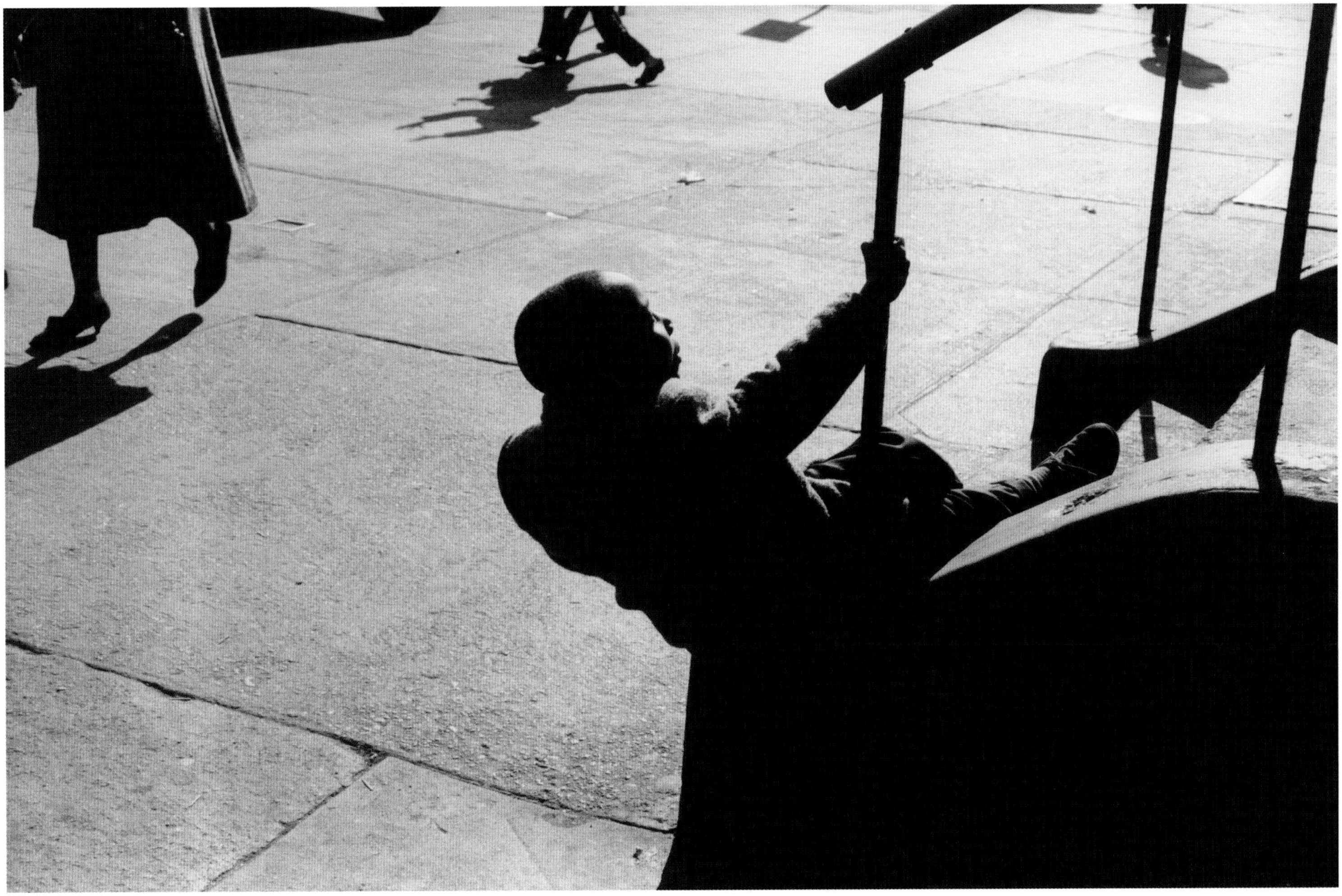

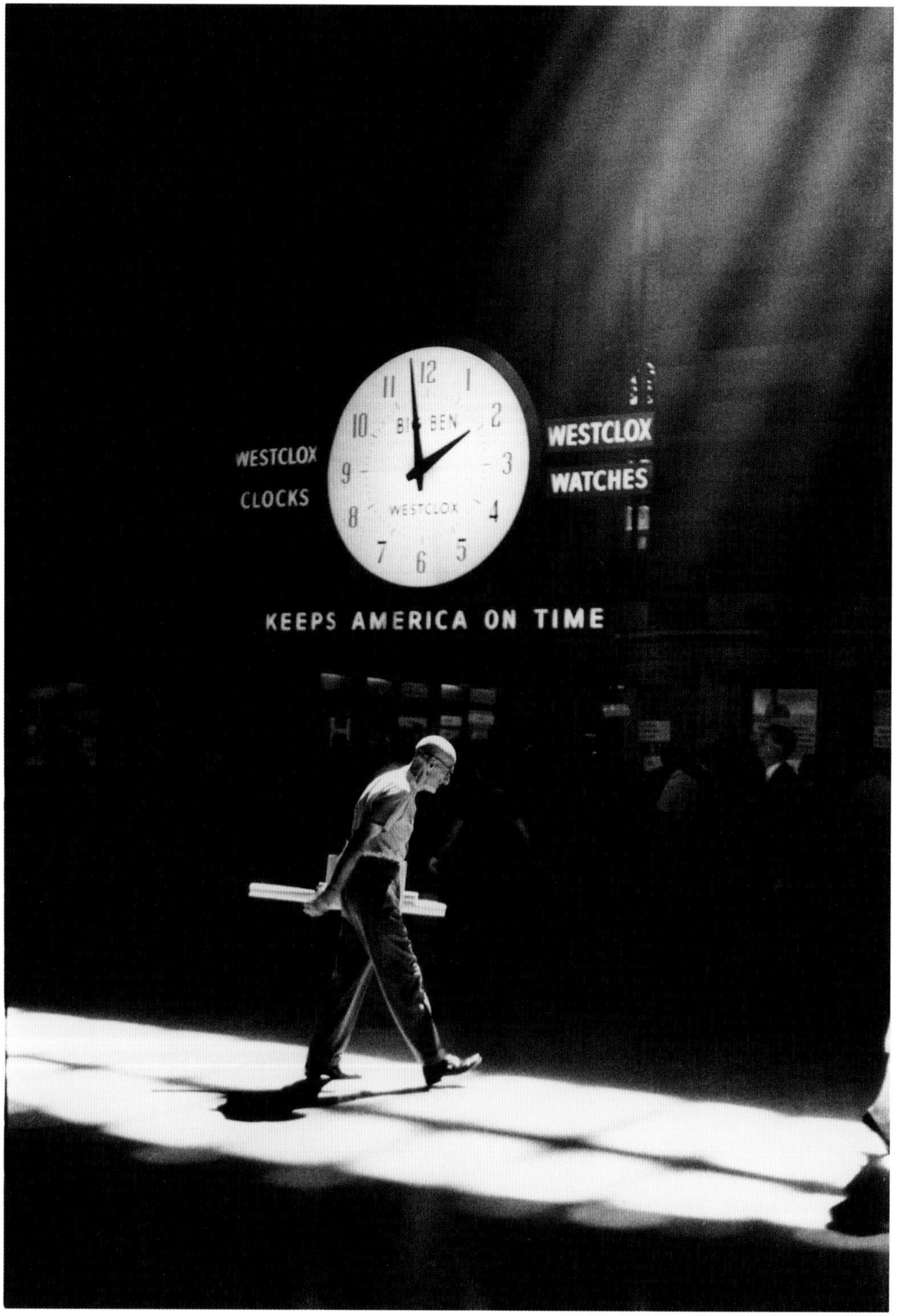

WESTCLOX
CLOCKS
BIG BEN
WESTCLOX
WESTCLOX
WATCHES
KEEPS AMERICA ON TIME

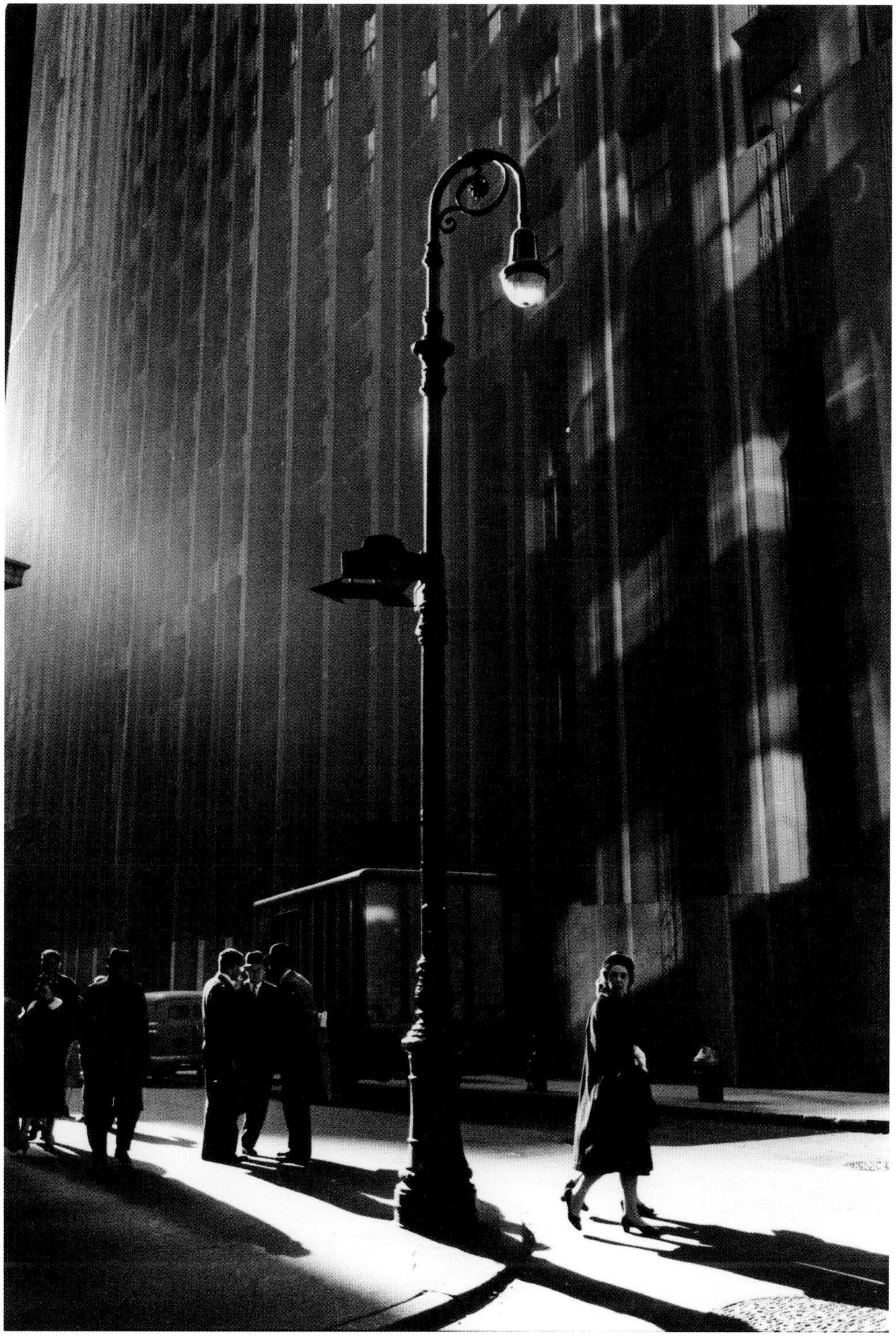

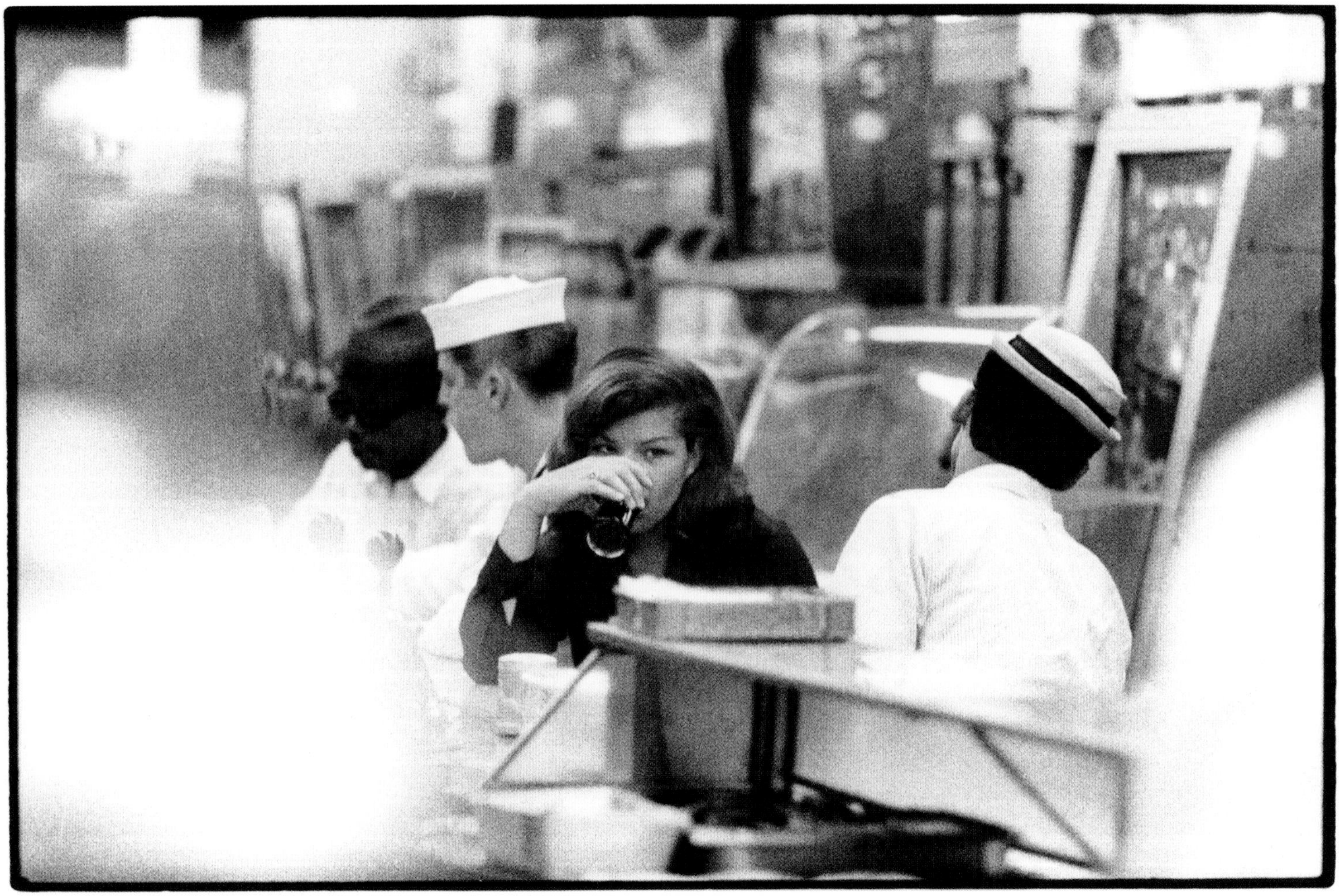

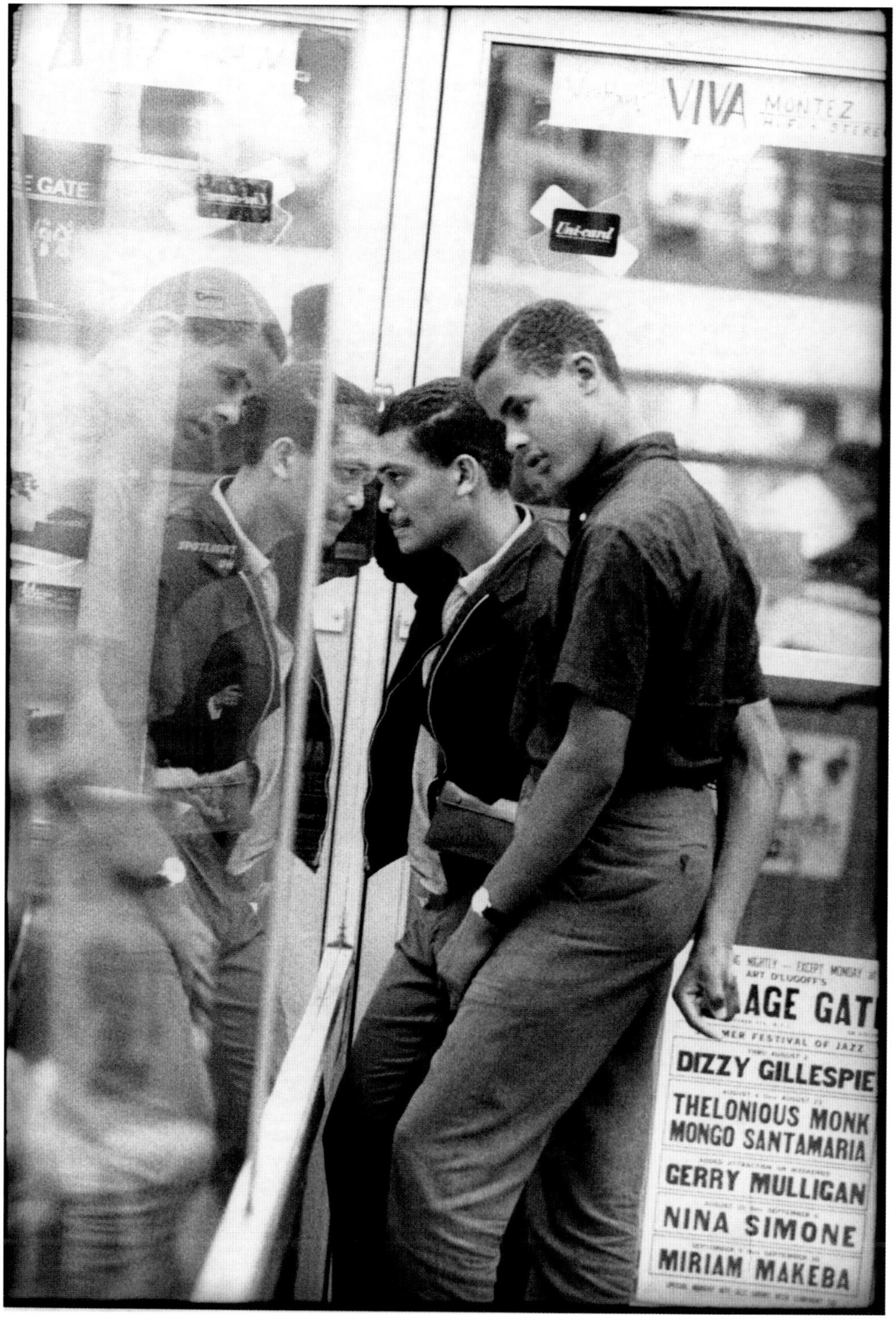
VIVA
MONTEZ
AGE GAT
MER FESTIVAL OF JAZZ
DIZZY GILLESPIE
THELONIOUS MONK
MONGO SANTAMARIA
GERRY MULLIGAN
NINA SIMONE
MIRIAM MAKEBA

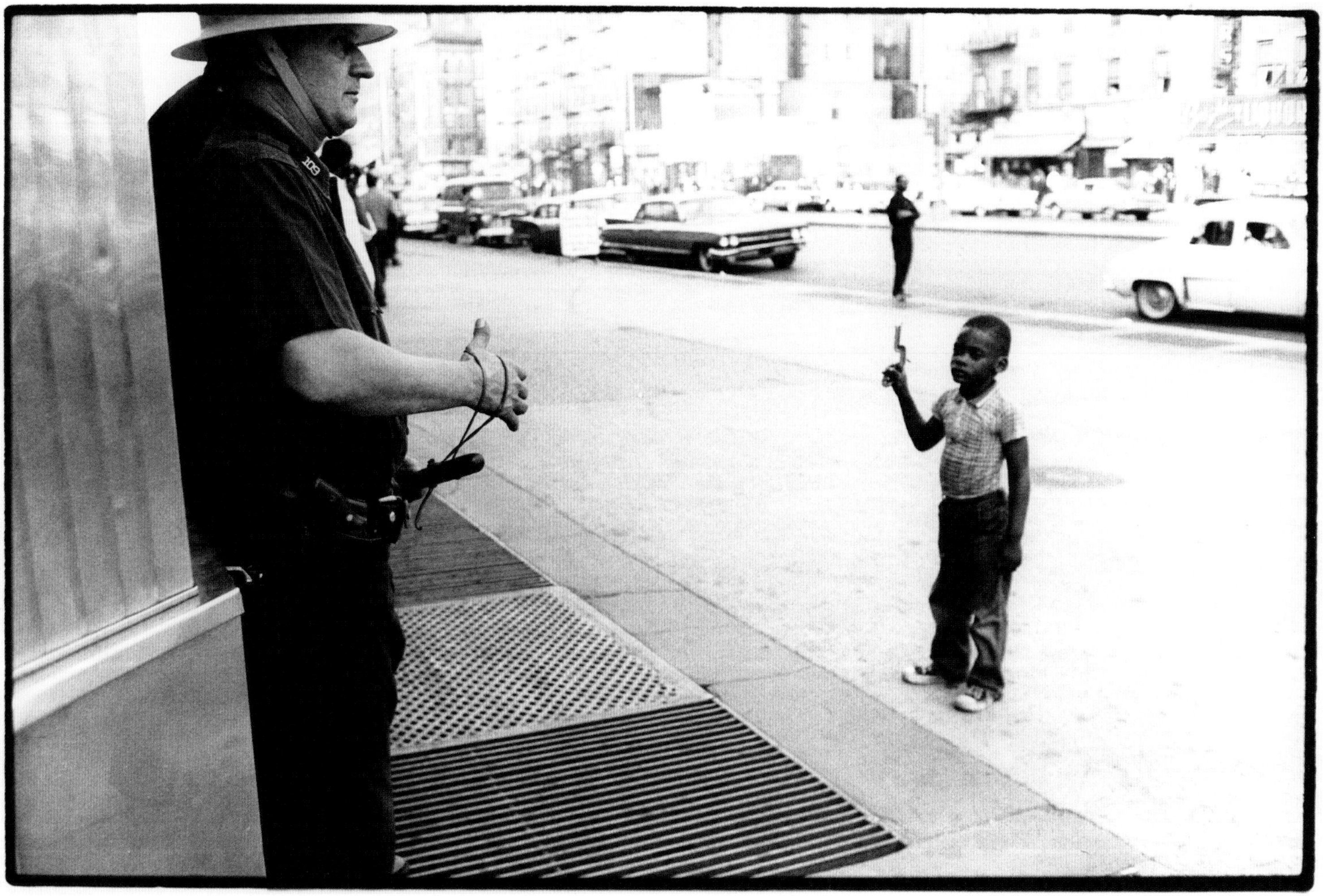

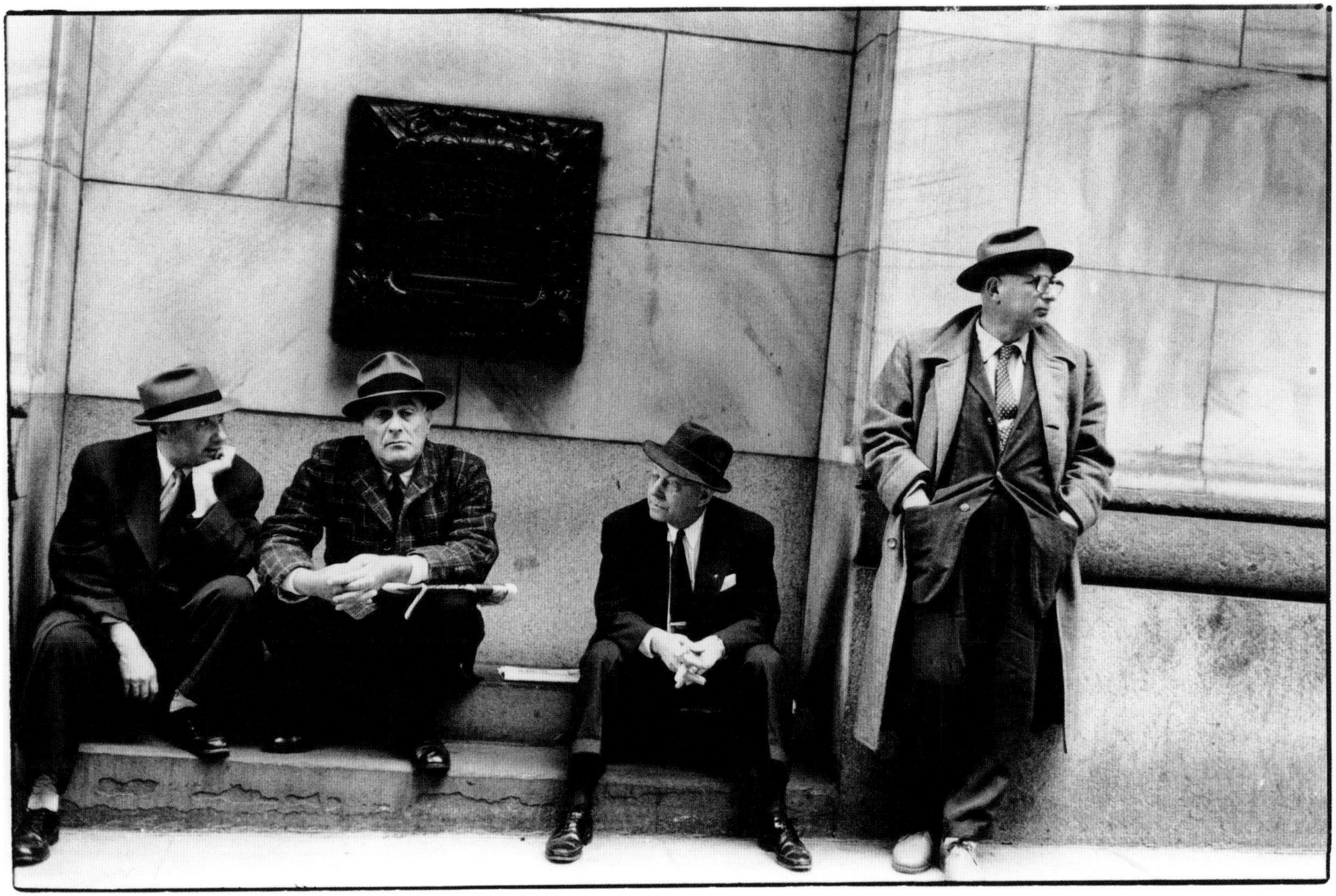

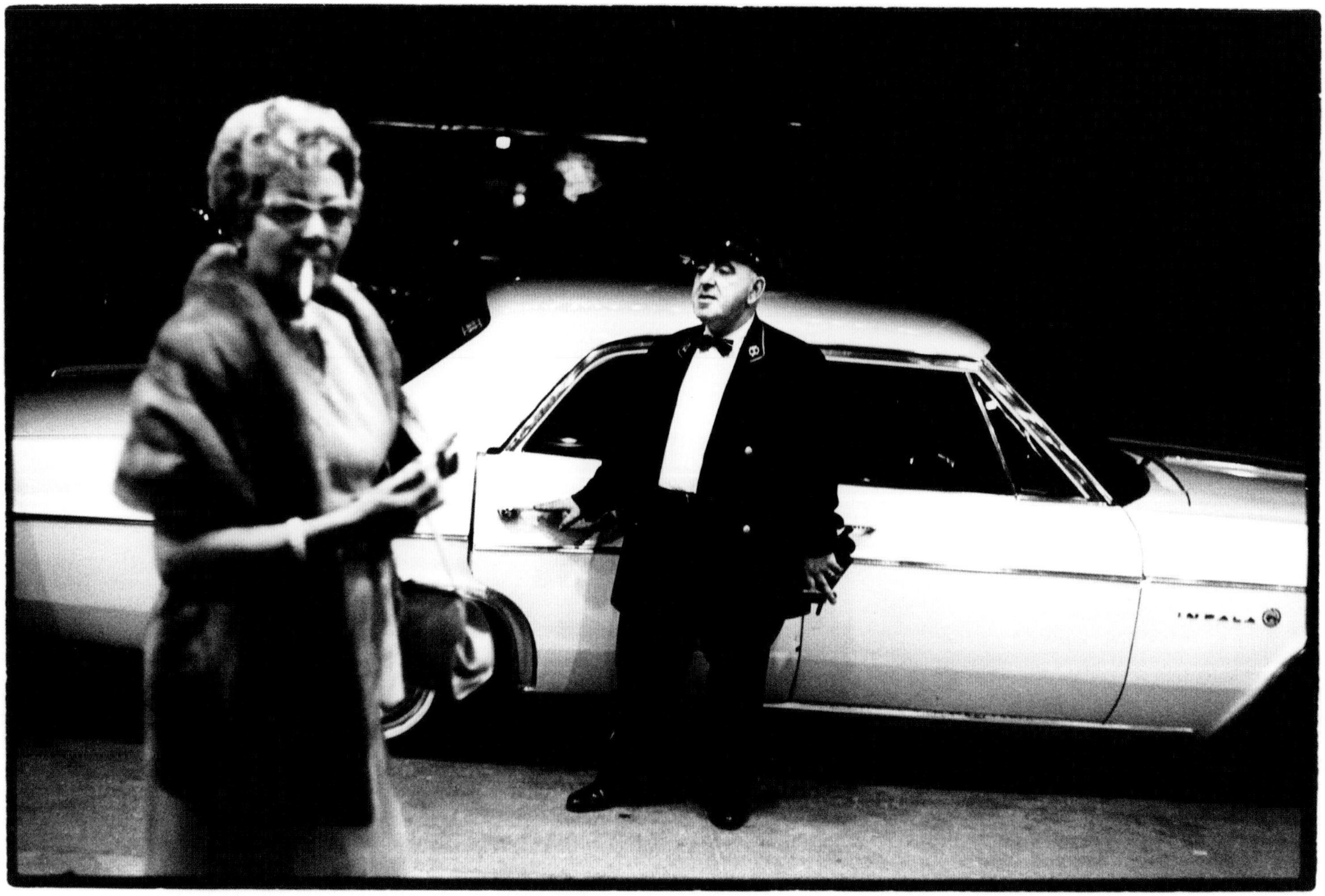
IMPALA

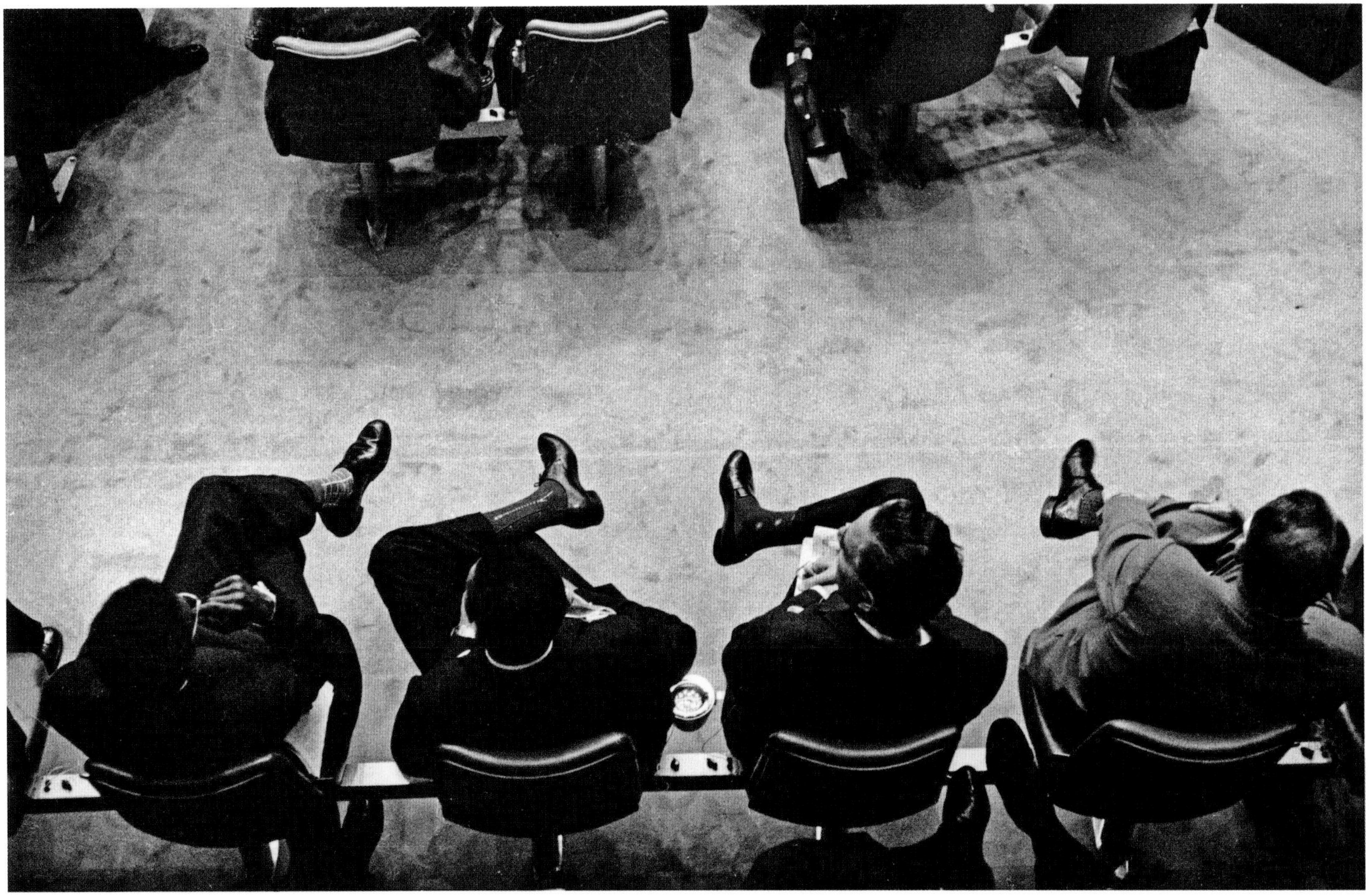

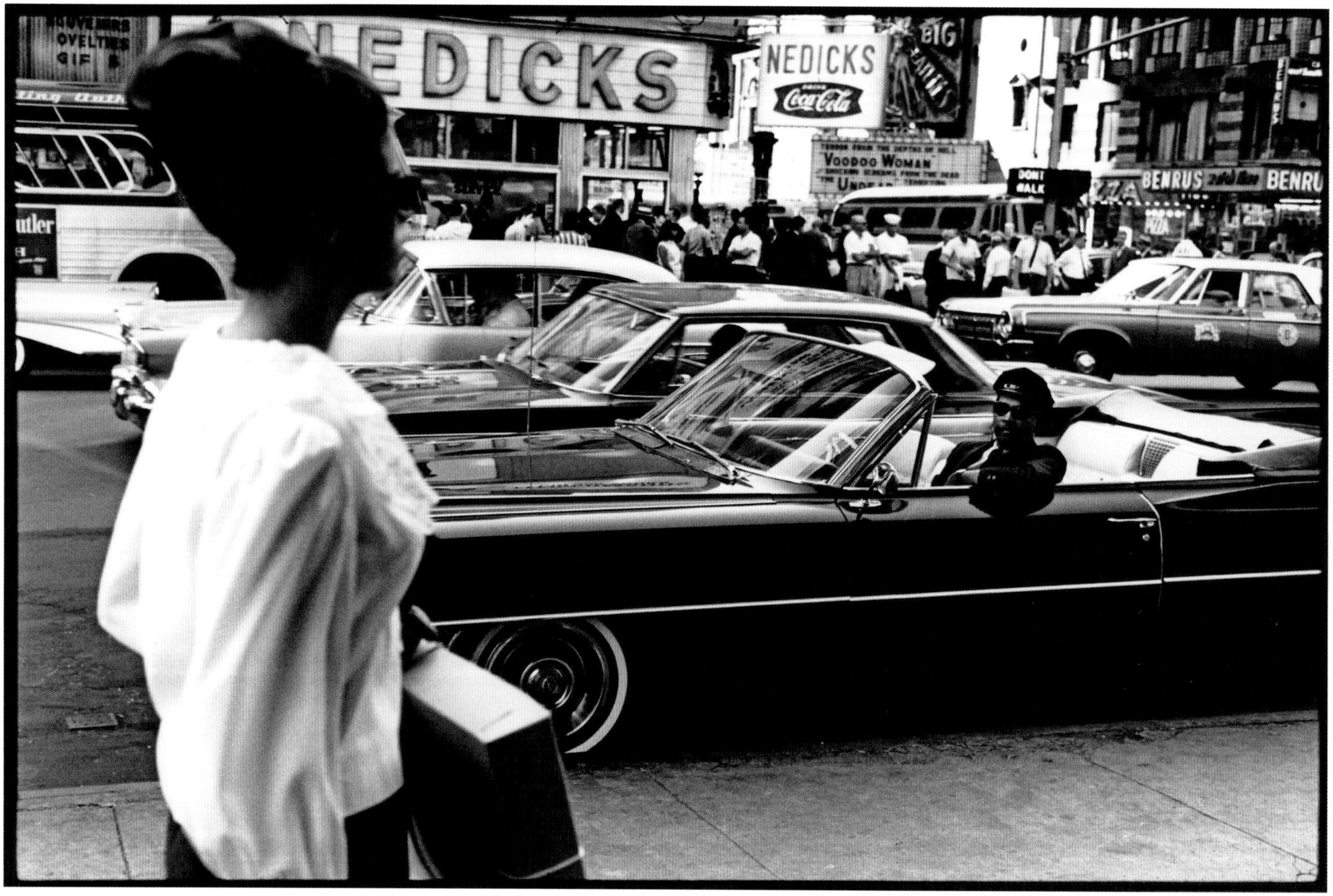
NEDICKS
NEDICKS
Coca-Cola
VOODOO WOMAN
BENRUS

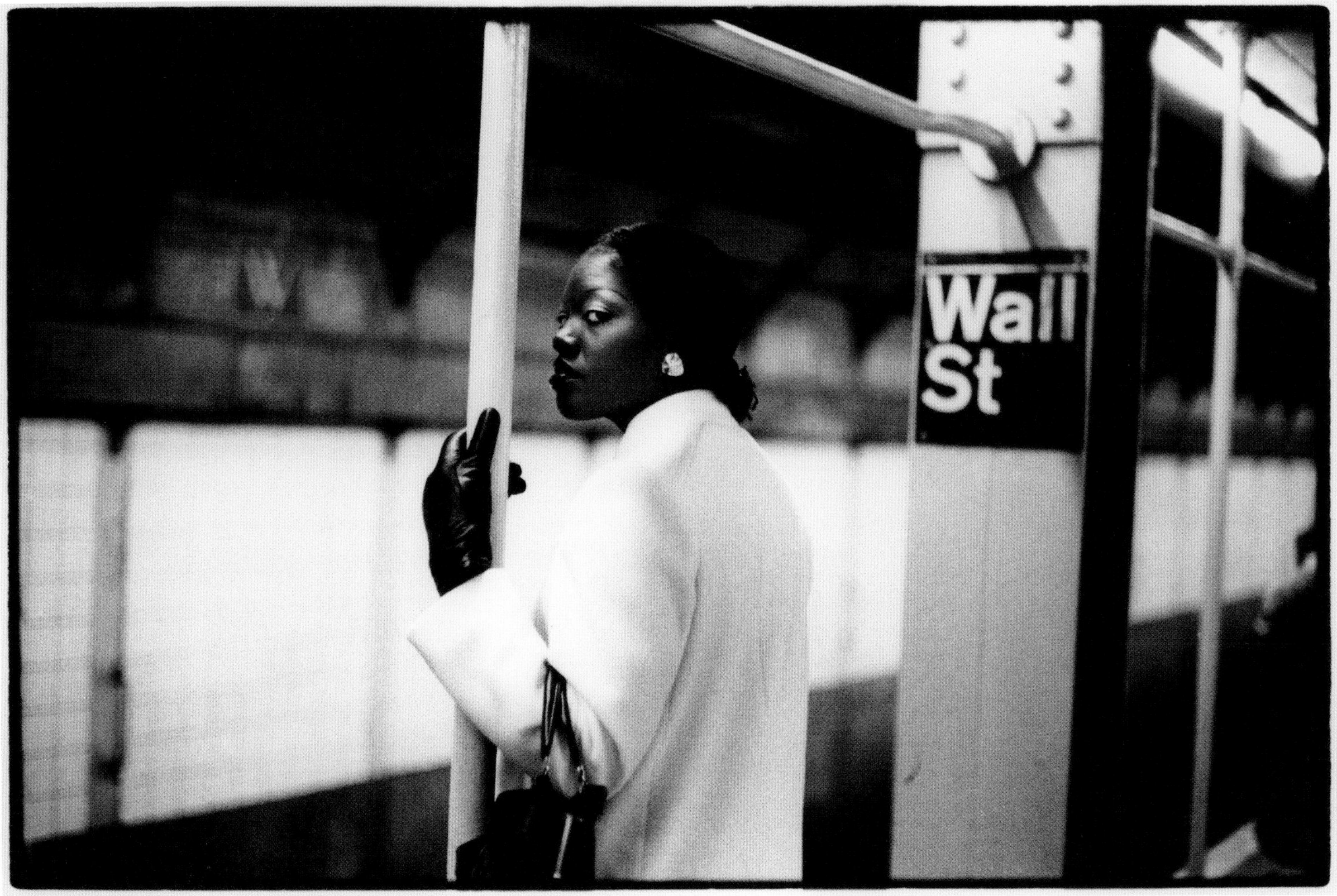
Wall
St

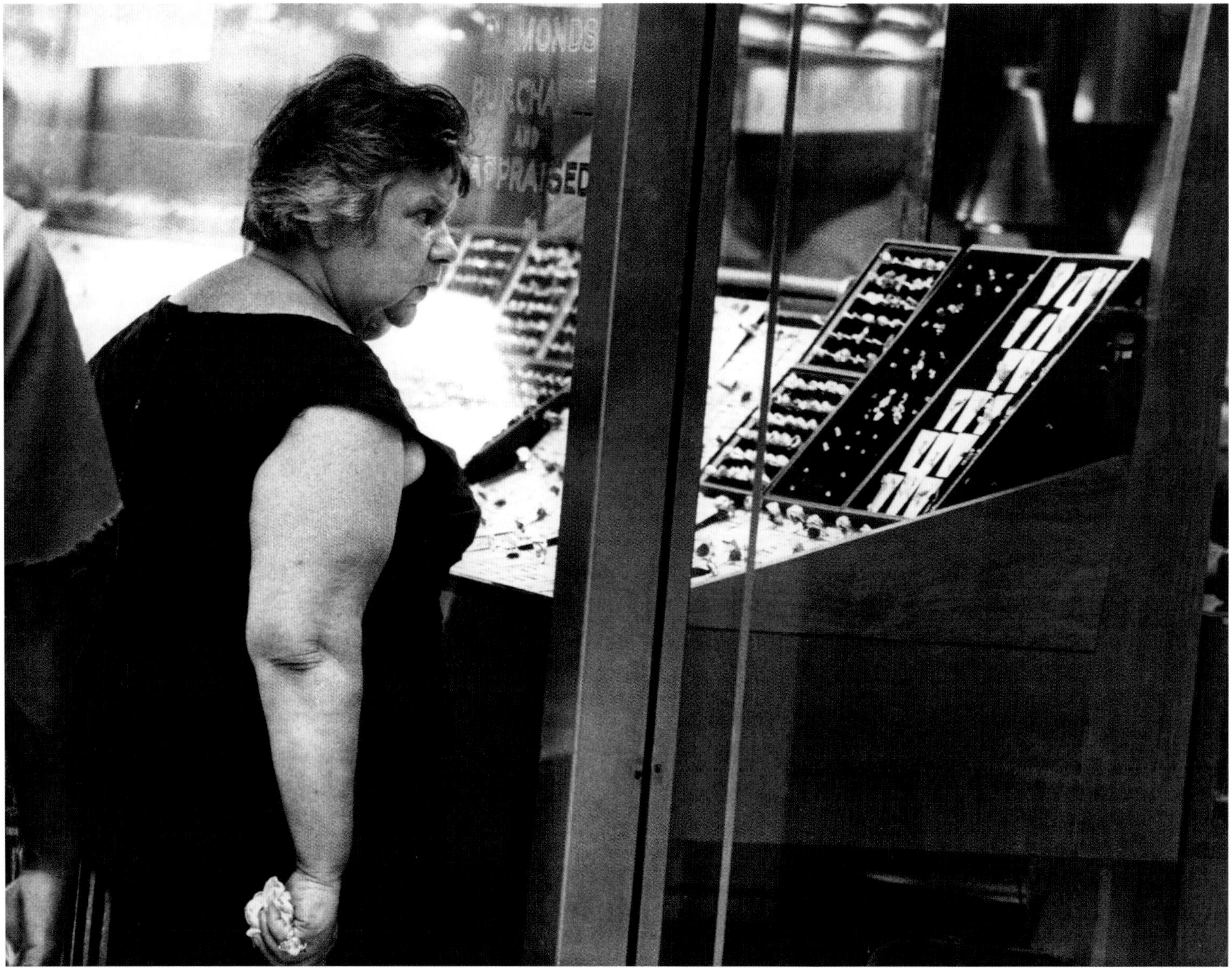
MONDS
PURCHA
AND
PPRAISED

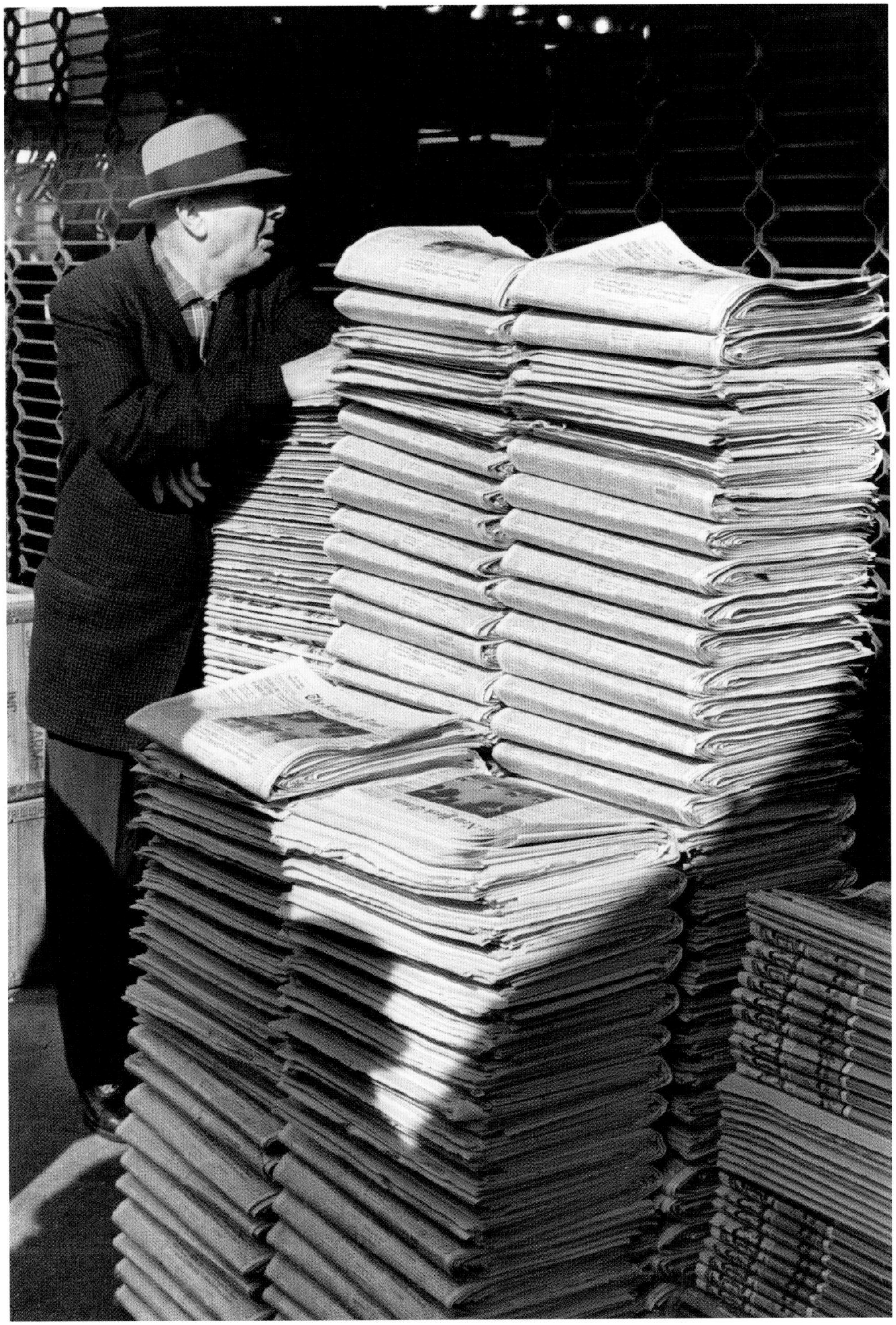

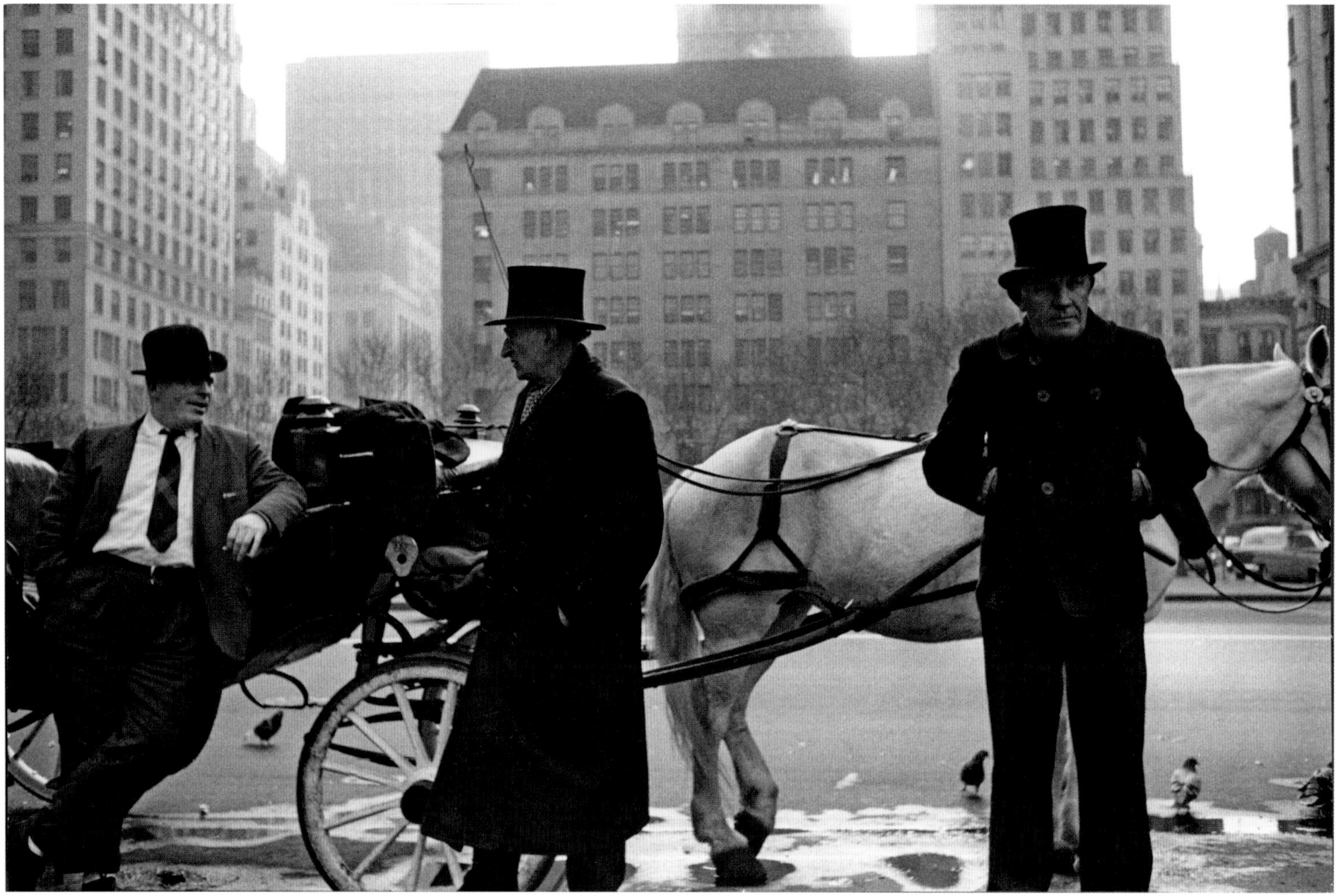

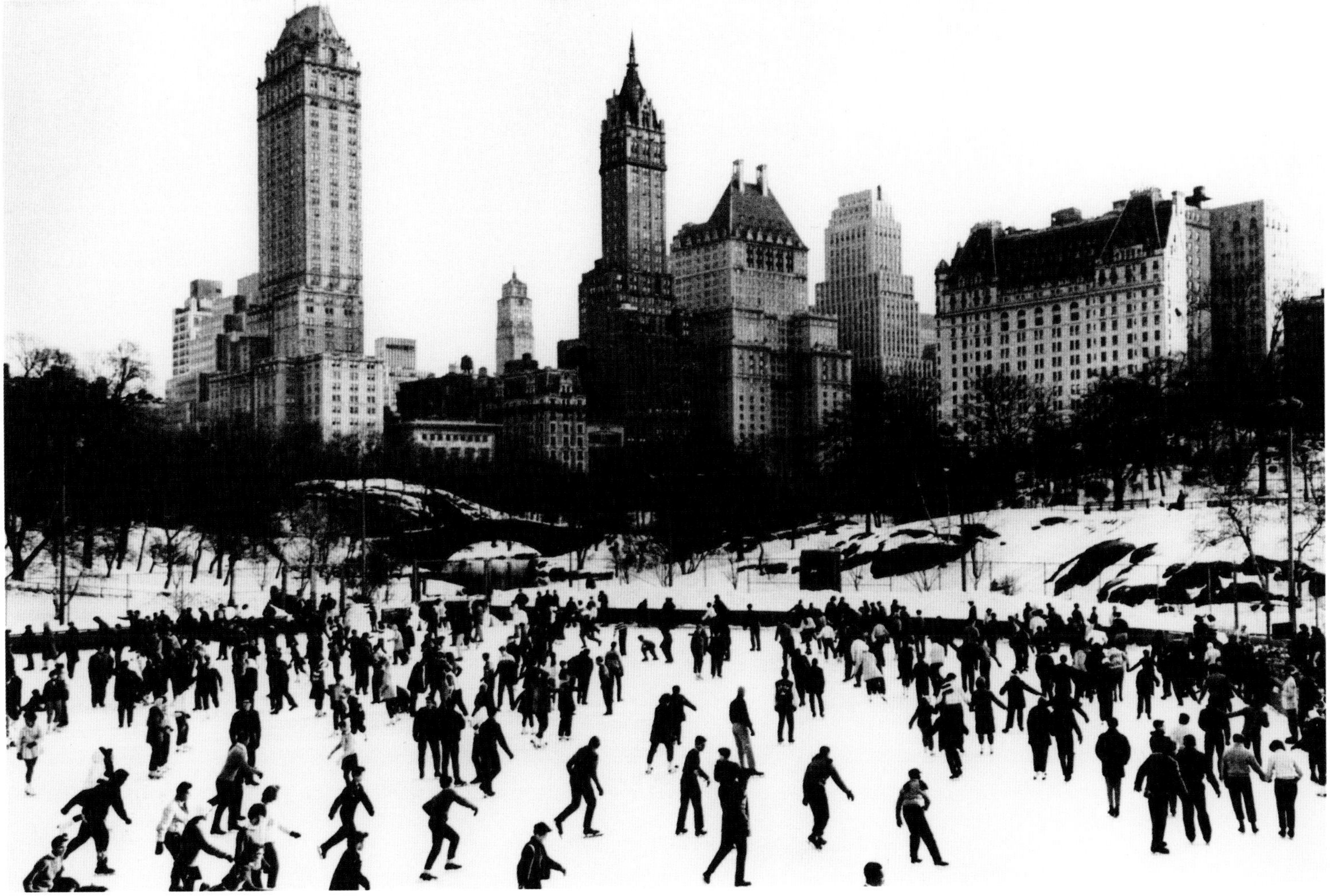

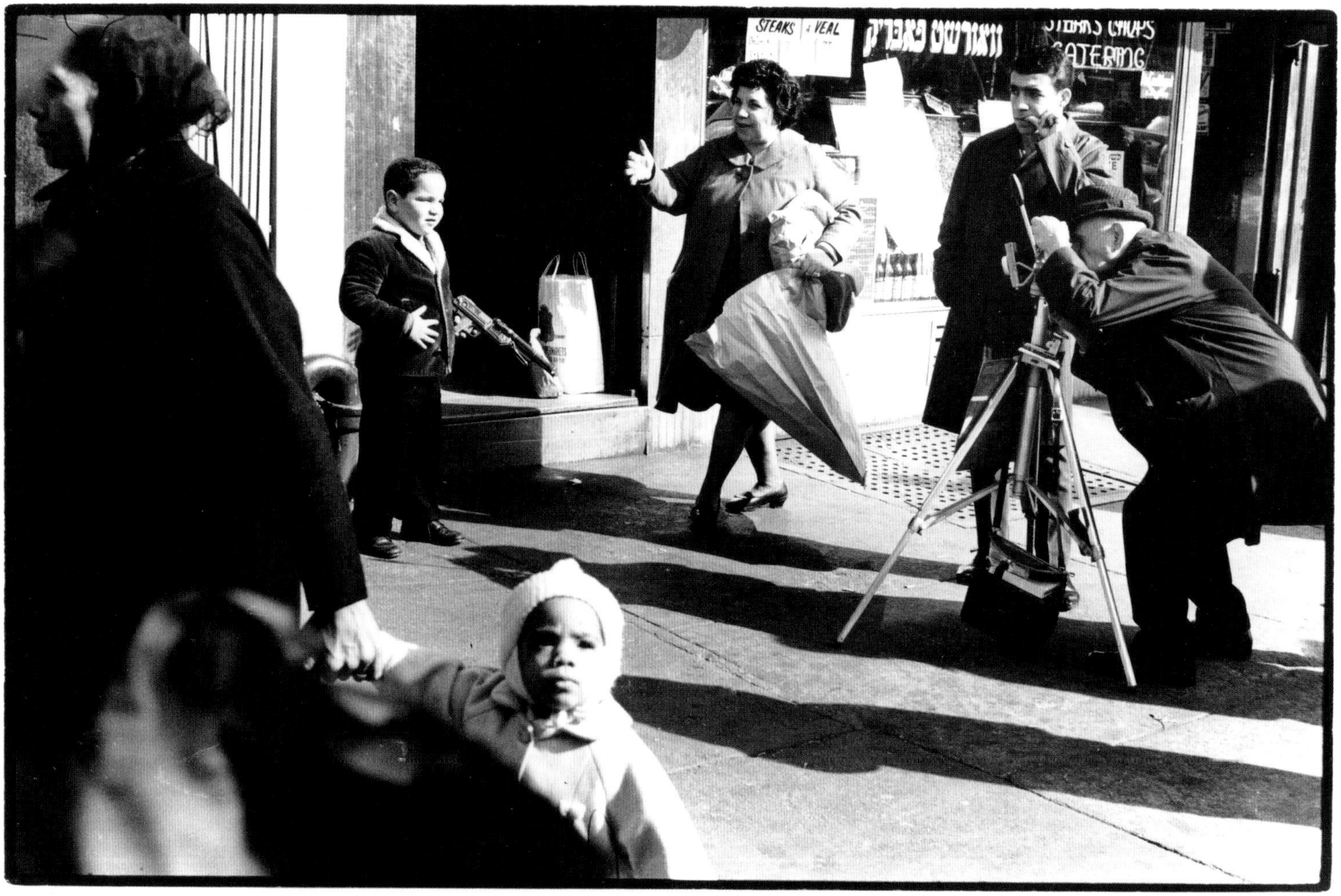
STEAKS
VEAL
וואורשט פאבריק
CATERING

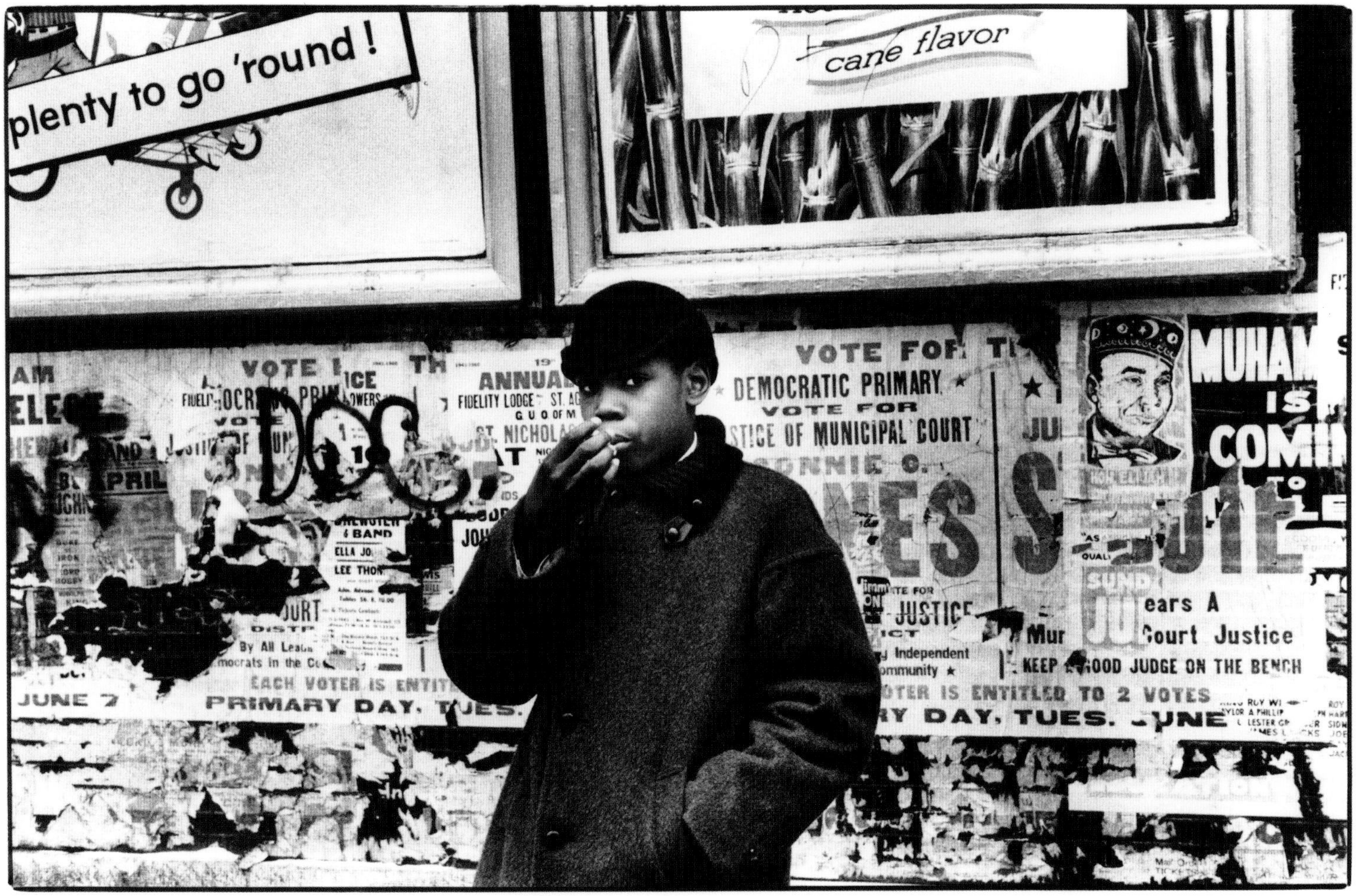
plenty to go 'round !
cane flavor
VOTE FOR
DEMOCRATIC PRIMARY
VOTE FOR
ANNUAL
FIDELITY LODGE
ST. NICHOLAS
ELLA JO
LEE THOM
By All Leag
EACH VOTER IS ENTIT
JUNE 7
PRIMARY DAY, TUES.
JUSTICE
Independent
Community
OTER IS ENTITLED TO 2 VOTES
RY DAY, TUES. JUNE
HON. ELIJAH
MUHAM
IS
COMIN
ears A
Court Justice
KEEP A GOOD JUDGE ON THE BENCH

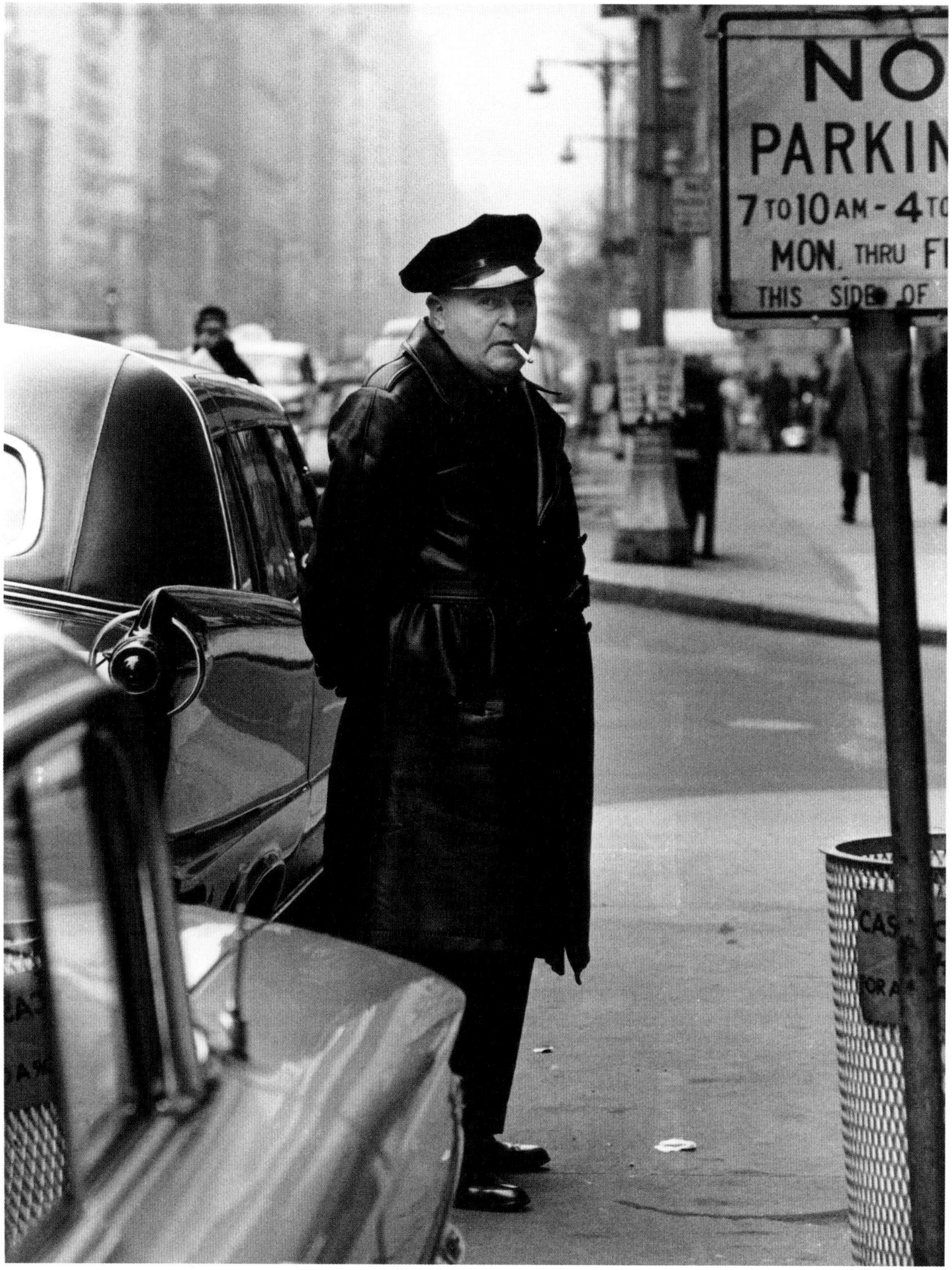
NO
PARKIN
7 TO 10 AM - 4 TO
MON. THRU F
THIS SIDE OF

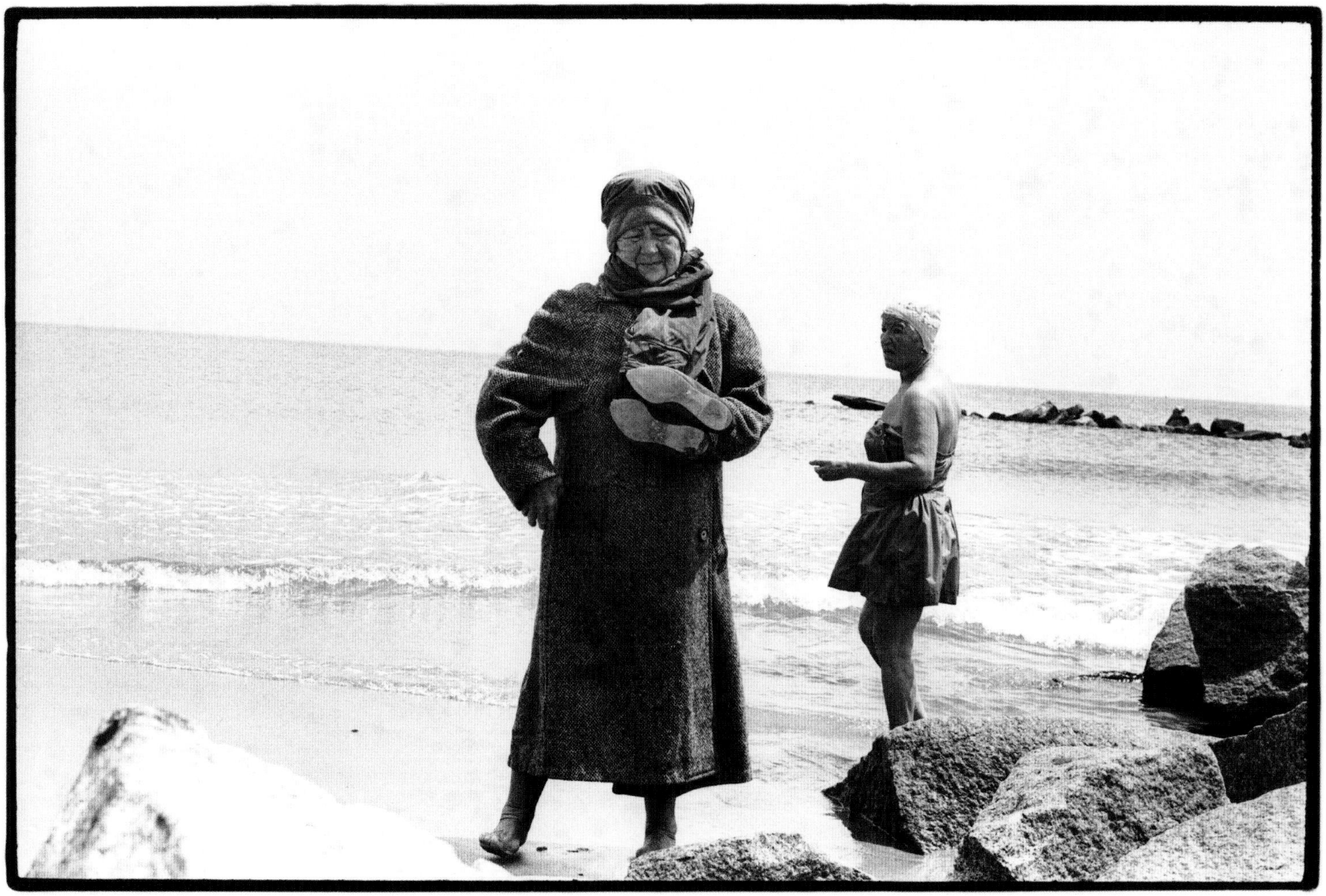

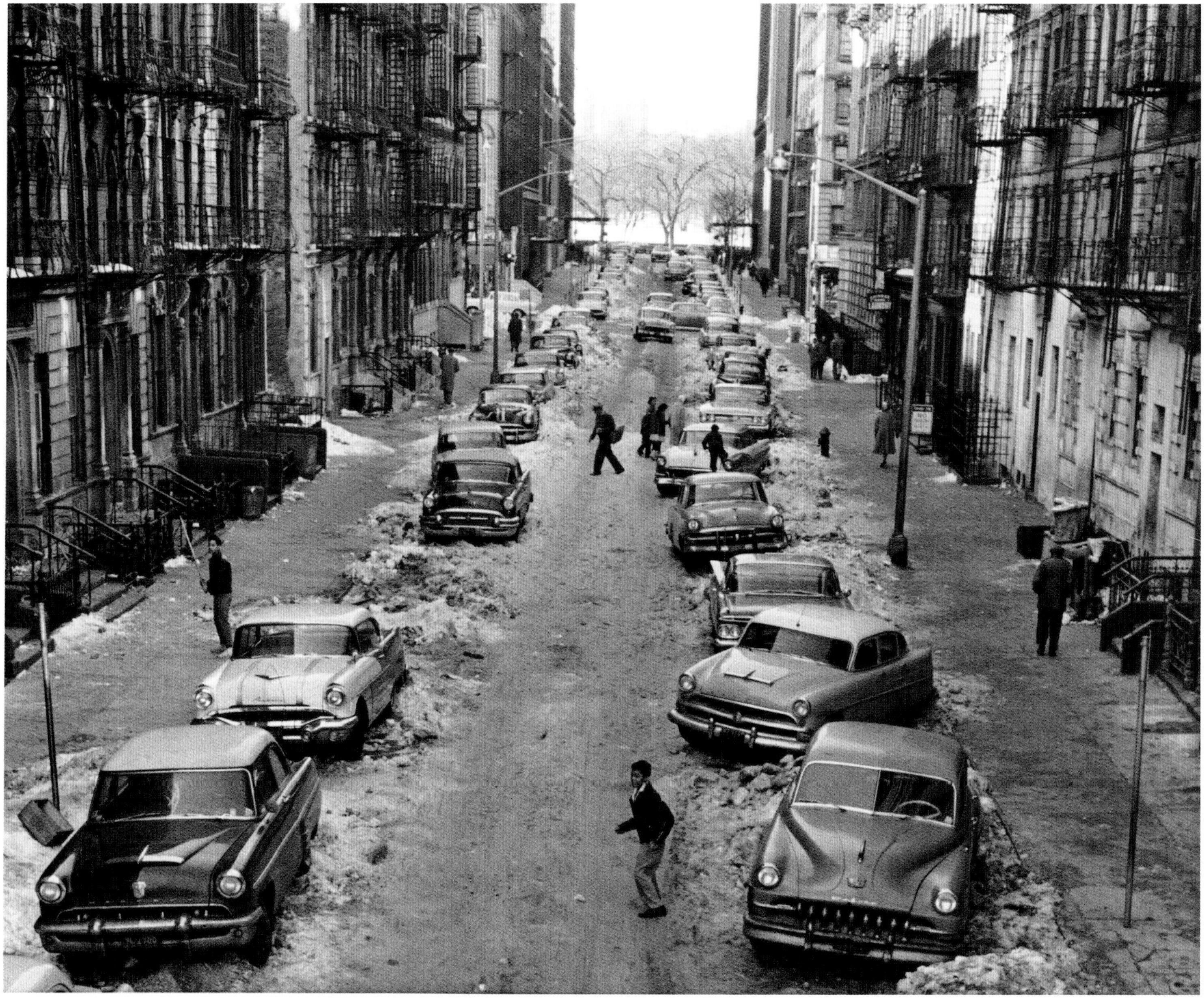

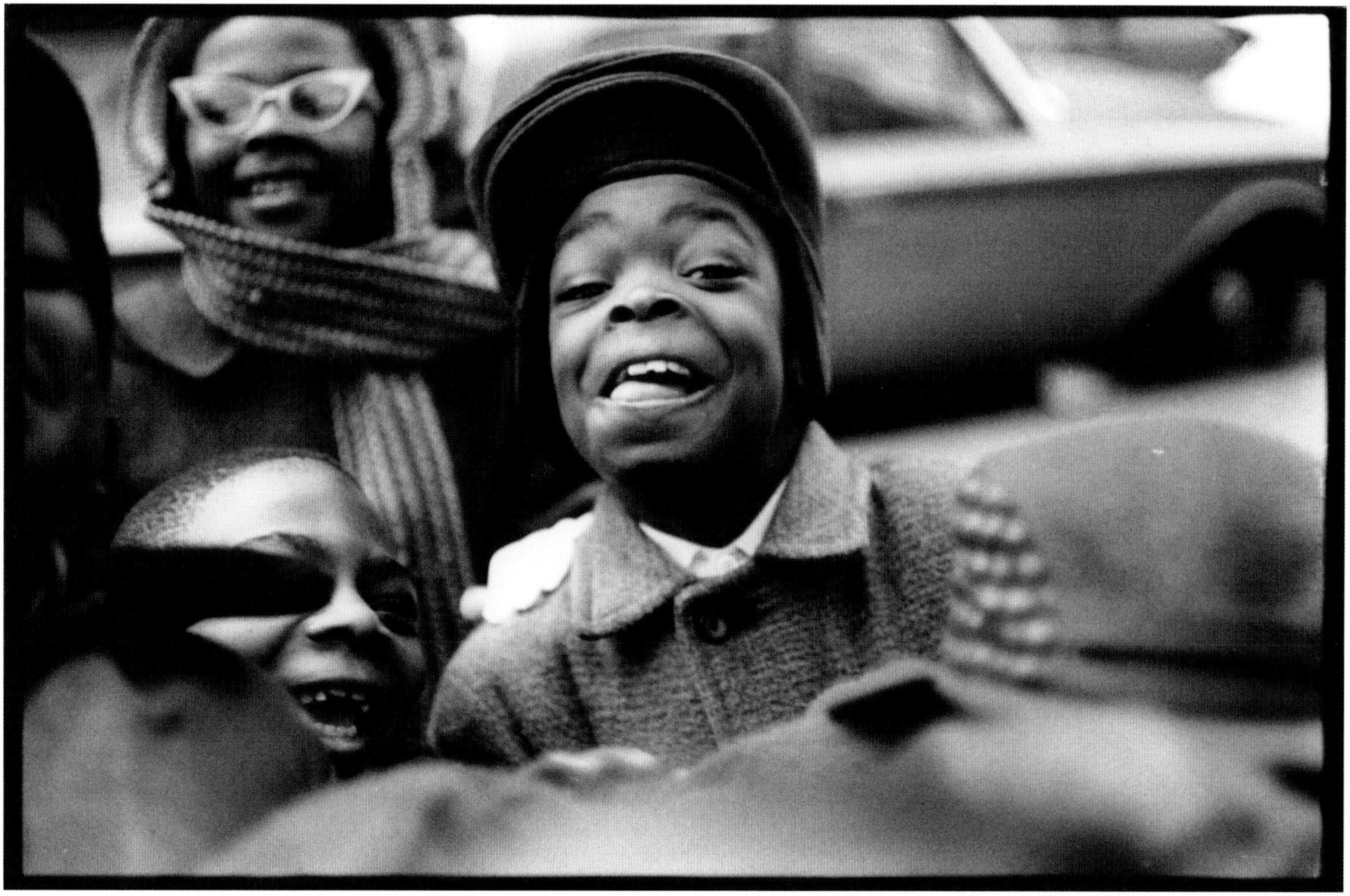

List of Works

All prints are silver gelatin

Wolf Suschitzky

Charing Cross Road, c.1937, pp. 8, 26
Milkman on the Charing Cross Road, 1935, p. 27
Charing Cross Road, 1936, pp. 22, 28
Charing Cross Road, 1936, pp. 19, 29
'Second Front' Meeting, Trafalgar Square, 1942, p. 30
Charing Cross Road, c.1936, p. 31
Casimir Beltrami, Knife-grinder, Charing Cross Road, 1937, p. 32
Cambridge Circus, 1936, p. 33
St Paul's, c.1942, p. 34
View from St Paul's Cathedral, August 1942, p. 35
VE Day, Coventry Street, Piccadilly Circus, 1945, p. 36
Blind Man, c.1936, p. 37
Sheep in Hyde Park, 1934, p. 38
Charing Cross Road, c.1934, p. 39
The Largest Photograph, Monument Station, 1938, p. 40
Cambridge Circus, 1936, p. 41
The Weekly Milk Bill, Charing Cross Road, 1937, p. 42
War in Wax, Oxford Street, 1945, p. 43
Queue outside Wyndham's Theatre, 1934, p. 44
Charing Cross Road, 1936, p. 45, back cover

Dorothy Bohm

Quai du Louvre, Paris, 1952, p. 54
Villa des Tulipes, 18th arrondissement, near the Marché aux Puces, 1953, p. 55
Paris, 1958, p. 56
Paris, 1955, p. 57
Near the Old Les Halles Market, 1953, p. 58
Boulevard Saint-Michel, entrance to the Luxembourg Gardens, 1955, p. 59
Rue Tholozé, Montmartre, 1954, p. 60, back cover
Place du Tertre, Montmartre, 1950, pp. 2, 61
Paris, 1947, p. 62
Montmartre, 1952, p. 63
Twins, Villa des Tulipes, 18th arrondissement, near the Marché aux Puces, 1953, p. 64
Goat Carriage, Tuileries Gardens, 1953, p. 65
Tuileries Gardens, 1953, p. 66
Antique Shop, Rue La Boétie, 1956, p. 67
The Seine, Quai du Louvre and Pont-Neuf, 1955, p. 68
The Seine and the Île de la Cité, from the Quai du Louvre, under the Pont des Arts, 1955, pp. 48, 69
Trois Maillets Museum, Rue Saint-Julien-le-Pauvre and Rue Galande, 1955, p. 70
Place du Tertre in Winter, 1952, p. 71

Neil Libbert

Harlem, 1960, pp. 6, 78
Children of Harlem, 1960, p. 79
Grand Central Station, 1960, p. 80
Wall Street, 1960, pp. 81, 101
Bar on 42nd Street, 1960, p. 82
42nd Street, 1960, p. 83
Harlem Race Riots, 1964, p. 84
Wall Street, 1960, p. 85
Nightlife, Broadway, 1960, p. 86
UN General Assembly, 1960, p. 87
42nd Street, 1960, p. 88
Wall Street, 1968, p. 89, cover
Diamond District, 47th Street, 1964, p. 90
Newsvendor, 1964, p. 91
Cabbies and Horses, 1960, p. 92
New York City Skyline, from Central Park, 1960, p. 93
Lower East Side, 1964, p. 94
Harlem Boy, 1960, p. 95
Chauffeur, 1960, p. 96, back cover
Coney Island Paddle, 1964, p. 97
East 98th Street, Harlem, 1960, p. 98
Harlem, 1960, pp. 75, 99

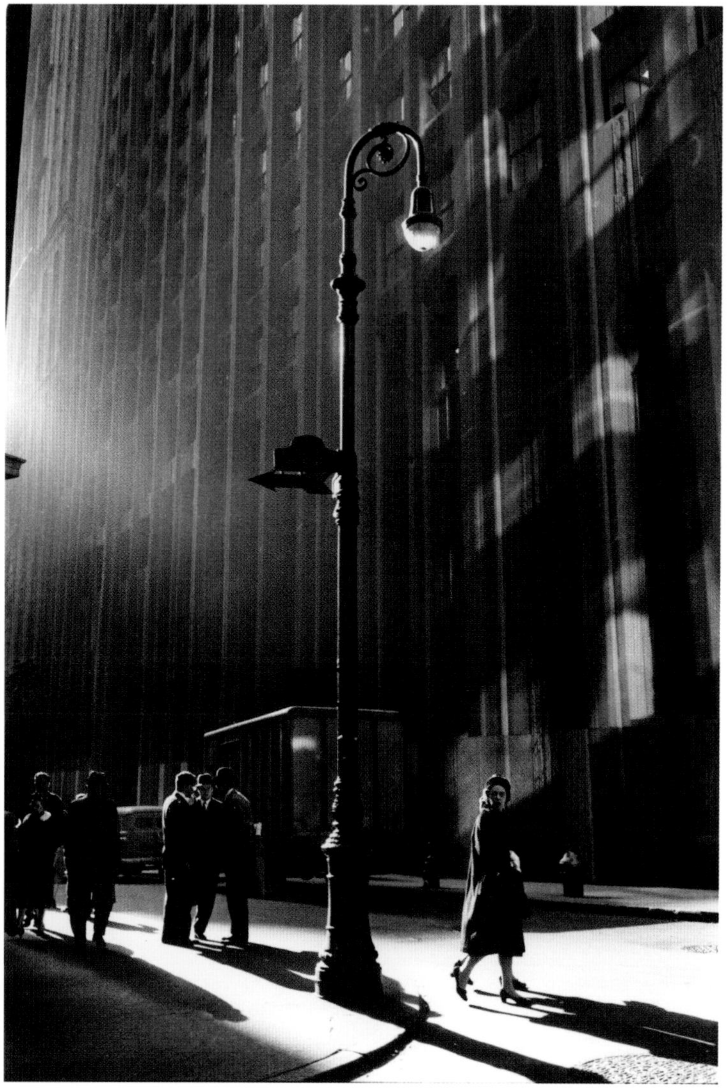

Biographies

Saskia Rubin

Wolf Suschitzky

Born in 1912, Wolf Suschitzky grew up in Vienna within one of the city's most prominent social-democratic families. His father, Wilhelm Suschitzky, was the co-founder with his brother of a socialist bookshop and publishing house in the working-class district of Favoriten. The social activism of his family and their circle, which involved an emphasis on free-thinking and the extensive consumption of literature, would have a profound effect on the subjects that Wolf would capture throughout his working life.

Owing to his parents' belief in the principles of communal living, Suschitzky was sent to a progressive boarding school in Vienna, where he gained an excellent, well-rounded education. It was Wolf's elder sister, Edith Suschitzky (later Tudor Hart), who inspired him to specialise in photography upon graduation from school. Edith was trained at the Bauhaus school late in the 1920s and later forged a distinguished career in the United Kingdom as a documentary photographer.

Wolf's formal training took place at the Höhere Graphische Bundes-Lehr- und Versuchsanstalt in Vienna. Despite what he perceived to be a considerable neglect of 'the aesthetic aspects of photography' within the three-year course, Suschitzky benefitted from a rigorous technical training, which included 'developing by inspection, bromide paper printing' and 'optics and chemistry'.[1]

The outbreak of civil war in 1934, which followed a period of rising nationalism and anti-Semitism in Austria, forced Suschitzky to flee from Vienna – an essential move given his family's political outlook and secular Jewish roots. Initially, he joined his sister Edith in London, where she had married a communist doctor and gained full citizenship. Wolf brought with him a fellow photography student from Vienna, Pucky Voûte, whom he married at Hampstead Town Hall soon after arriving on British soil. Unable to gain work permits, the newlyweds moved to Pucky's native Amsterdam and set up a photography studio in their flat.

A little over a year later, a disintegrated marriage behind him, Suschitzky returned to London with renewed determination to establish a career there. He helped his sister on commercial projects and worked as a freelance photographer. In 1937 he remained without a work permit and thus volunteered as a camera assistant at Strand Films, run by pioneering documentary maker Paul Rotha. This period saw the production of many of Suschitzky's most famous photographs of London, including the much-displayed Charing Cross Road series, some of which feature in this exhibition. Furthermore, it marked the beginning of Suschitzky's successful career as a documentary cinematographer.

Making films presented Suschitzky with invaluable access to sights that were usually restricted from public view. He was commissioned to film in locations that were scattered not only throughout the United Kingdom, but also worldwide. He took still photographs alongside filming, becoming an Associate of the Royal Photographic Society by 1940, and producing regular work for *Illustrated London News*, *Lilliput*, *The Listener*, *Picture Post*, *Animal and Zoo* and *Geographical Magazine*. During the Second World War Suschitzky travelled around the United Kingdom, making films for the Ministry of Information. He thus gained entry to a variety of organisations such as steelworks, hospitals and factories. This provided fertile ground for socially poignant photography, which was in line with the principles instilled in Wolf from his upbringing in Vienna.

Suschitzky's commissions for the National Broadcasting Company (NBC) in the United States, dating from the 1950s, took him across continents, where he met leading politicians and renowned public figures. One such example was *Assignment India*, produced by Robert Graff and broadcast in November of 1955. During this project, Suschitzky filmed an interview with Jawaharlal Nehru and grasped the opportunity to capture the Prime Minister in a series of intimate portraits. The sponsorship of NBC also sent Wolf to Indonesia, Thailand and Burma.

Wolf Suschitzky's photography has been exhibited widely throughout his career. Museums that have displayed his work include the Photographers' Gallery, the Open Eye Gallery, Liverpool, the Scottish National Gallery and the Kunsthalle Wien.

[1] Wolf Suschitzky, 'A Short Autobiography of a Long-lived Photographer', in *Wolf Suschitzky Photos*, edited by Brigitte Mayr, Michael Omasta and Ursula Seeber (Vienna: Synema, 2006), p. 196.

Dorothy Bohm

Dorothy Bohm began life in 1924 as Dorothea Israelit, in the coastal town of Königsberg in East Prussia (now Kaliningrad, Russia). She was born into a prosperous Jewish family, her father Tobias having established a thriving textiles business. The Israelit family moved to Memel in 1932, in order to distance themselves from the increasingly threatening spread of Nazism, a move which offered them protection for seven years. In March of 1939, only months before the outbreak of the Second World War, and a single day before the Nazis stormed Memel, the Israelits fled east to the city of Šiauliai. In June, Dorothy was sent alone to the United Kingdom. As Tobias placed his prized Leica around her neck at the train station, both were unaware that they would endure a separation of over twenty years.

Learning English from scratch, Dorothy attended a small school in Ditchling, Sussex. Discouraged by the costly fees and lengthy training involved in becoming a doctor, Dorothy decided to study photography. She was drawn to the North of England by the fact that her brother Igor was already a student at Manchester College of Technology, and in 1940 she took up a vocational course in photography at the same institution. The two-year programme was fundamentally technical, and Dorothy worked hard alongside it to obtain a City & Guilds certificate, which usually required four years of preparation.

Following her graduation from the College of Technology, with the top photography prize for portraiture under her belt, Dorothy was invited to teach evening classes at her *alma mater*. During her studies she met her future husband, Louis Bohm, a chemistry student and Polish-Jewish émigré. Early in the 1940s Louis introduced her to Marie Nordlinger, an older artist who was renowned for her central role in the Manchester Arts and Crafts movement, and for her close relationship with Marcel Proust, which dated back to her painting studies in Paris at the turn of the twentieth century. Dorothy considered Nordlinger a true 'mentor'[1]; a strong woman whose 'account of Proustian Paris fired my imagination, made me want to learn, study, observe, travel, especially in France and Italy'.[2]

Before Dorothy's dreams of adventure were to be satisfied, she worked at Samuel Cooper's portrait studio in Manchester between 1942 and 1945. War was ongoing, and the demand for portraiture was high since it provided some semblance of closeness for the many families that were split apart. Her other major contribution to the British war effort, facilitated by the Ministry of Information, was to give regular talks on 'Europe under the Nazis'. Under the pseudonym Dorothy Alexander, a precaution taken to distance herself from her Jewish descent, Dorothy addressed audiences at factories, mining communities, church halls, libraries and rotary clubs, informing them of the evils of the Nazi regime. She even gave a lecture to the American Air Force in Blackpool on D-Day itself (6 June 1944).

In November 1945, soon after the war had ended, Dorothy married Louis Bohm. While her new husband was finishing a doctorate in chemistry, Dorothy proudly assumed the role of breadwinner. She opened her own photography premises, Studio Alexander, at 28–30 Market Street in Manchester. The portrait studio would remain a valuable source of income up until Bohm sold it in 1958. Dogged determination saw Dorothy past a number of practical hurdles at the outset of her business. Most challenging was the post-war shortage of furniture and materials such as film, paper and chemicals.

Dorothy's thirst for travel was first satisfied in 1947, when she and Louis made a trip to Montreux in Switzerland to investigate a photographic studio that had come up for sale. Although the studio proved unsuitable, the young couple took the opportunity to travel on the continent. Dorothy's first glimpse of Paris was at the interchange between trains at the Gare de Lyon, en route to Switzerland. Decisive for her career was their stay in Ascona, a small fishing village on Lake Maggiore in the Ticino district of Switzerland. She likened it to 'paradise for living and for photography'.[3] During the slower periods at Studio Alexander, Dorothy returned repeatedly to Ascona. She revelled in its natural beauty and changing light, and felt liberated by photographing outdoors, capturing street scenes and landscapes alike. The community of international artists and intellectuals in Ascona, in particular the painter Otto Bachman and the sculptor Paul Vogt, also had a profound effect on Dorothy.

The 1950s would bring many further opportunities for travel. Louis Bohm had obtained his doctorate in chemistry, and was employed by a petrochemical company, initially in Manchester and then at their London branch. His job took him around Europe and North America, and Dorothy was fortunate to accompany him on his travels. In 1954, he was transferred to Paris, where the couple lived for one out of the three years that had been envisaged. Enamoured of her new surroundings, Dorothy endlessly explored the city where, for her, 'photography became an obsession'.[4] She also became friends with the artist Avigdor Arikha, who admired her photography and encouraged her to publish it.

After returning briefly to London, the Bohms went travelling around the United States and Mexico, both of which were rich in images for Dorothy to capture. In 1957, their stay in the United States came to an end and the Bohms found a flat in Hampstead. Their first daughter, Monica, was born, which made the continuation of Studio Alexander impractical. Their second daughter, Yvonne, arrived three years later. Dorothy's family life took an even more radical turn in 1960, when she travelled to the USSR to be reunited with her parents in Riga. She discovered that her father, mother and sister had miraculously survived internment at separate labour camps in Siberia where they had been prisoners since 1941. During this journey, Dorothy took photographs in Moscow and St Petersburg (then Leningrad). In 1963, through the intervention of Harold Wilson, the leader of the opposition in England, and with a significant amount of media attention, Dorothy gained permission for her parents to join her in England. Throughout this emotionally demanding period, Dorothy continued to take photographs, often in Sussex where her husband had purchased a working farm.

It was in 1969 that the Institute of Contemporary Arts put on the first exhibition displaying Bohm's work. The show, entitled *Spectrum – The Diversity of Photography – Four Photographers in Contrast*, included her photographs alongside those by Don McCullin, Tony Ray-Jones and Enzo Ragazzini. Her group of images, *People at Peace*, was juxtaposed with Don McCullin's presentation of *The Destruction Business*. Dorothy's eagerness to promote photography exhibitions in the United Kingdom led her to collaborate closely with Sue Davies in opening the Photographers' Gallery in 1971, the first public viewing space dedicated exclusively to the medium. As its Associate Director, she remained closely involved in the work of the gallery for fifteen years. Photographs taken on a family holiday to South Africa in 1974 resulted in a photography exhibition at the Photographers' Gallery in 1976.

The increased exposure of Dorothy's work to the public during the1970s expanded further in the 1980s, with a documentary about the photographer appearing on BBC2 in 1980 as part of the series *In the Making*. Beginning with an exploration of the colour Polaroid medium, promoted by her friend André Kertész in New York, the 1980s were important since they marked Dorothy's move from black and white to colour photography. The Far East was captured in vivid colour by Dorothy in 1984, and two visits to Egypt in 1985 and 1986 resulted in her first book of colour photographs. Her first colour prints were exhibited in 1986 at the Israel Museum in Jerusalem.

Dorothy continued to travel and to photograph, even after the death of her husband in 1994 during a trip to Ireland. Her work continues to be celebrated through solo shows at prestigious venues in London, including at Ben Uri,[5] Manchester, Paris and Berlin, and features in numerous private and public collections. She was elected an Honorary Fellow of the Royal Photographic Society in 2009; and her latest book, *About Women*, was published in 2015. Most importantly perhaps, at the age of nearly ninety-two, she is still taking photographs.

[1] Marika Cobbold and Amanda Hopkinson, *About Women: Photographs by Dorothy Bohm* (Stockport: Dewi Lewis Publishing, 2015), p. 10.

[2] Dorothy Bohm, 'A Memoir', in *Dorothy Bohm: Colour Photography*, introduction by Ian Jeffrey (London: Photographers' Gallery, 1994), p. 108.

[3] Bohm, 'A Memoir', p. 113.

[4] Colin Ford, 'Dorothy Bohm: A Life in Photography', in *A World Observed 1940–2010: Photographs by Dorothy Bohm*, texts by Monica Bohm-Duchen, Colin Ford and Ian Jeffrey (London: Philip Wilson Publishers, 2010), p. 16.

[5] *Ambiguous Realities: Colour Photographs by Dorothy Bohm*, exhibition at Ben Uri Gallery, London, 2006.

Neil Libbert

Neil Libbert was born in Salford in 1938 and moved one year later to live in Lytham St Annes, where he would remain until late adolescence.[1] He has been drawn to photography since childhood, and participated in the photographic societies within his school and local community.[2] Around the age of seventeen, Libbert took up a course in graphic design at the Regional College of Art in Manchester, and moved to the suburb of Didsbury. In 1957, following a year of studies, he opened his own photographic studio in Manchester, primarily taking portraits. The period spanning the late 1950s was especially formative for Neil, since he spent much of his time outside of the studio walking the streets of Salford and photographing children – a foretaste of the outdoor reportage for which he would become celebrated.[3]

The *Manchester Guardian* took Libbert on as a freelancer during the late 1950s and published his renowned series depicting the Manchester homeless in 1957. Addressing social themes has since been a leitmotif throughout Libbert's career, and is in line with the approach of Dorothea Lange (1895–1965) and Walker Evans (1903–1975), two photographers whom he greatly admires.[4] Neil joined the *Guardian* as a salaried member of staff around 1960. A decisive moment came in 1961, when the newspaper began to print in London and Neil moved to the capital – a development which he now deems 'a rather good idea'.[5] He worked for the *Guardian* until 1965, before signing contracts with the *Illustrated London News*, the *Sunday Times* and the *New York Times*.

In 1968, Libbert became a freelance photographer once again. His street photography has met with great acclaim, especially his coverage of the Brixton Riots in 1981. Libbert's exclusive photographs from the bomb attack at the Admiral Duncan Pub in Soho earned him the title of Nikon News Photographer of the Year, 1999. Until recent years, he also regularly covered performing arts photography for the *Observer*.

During his extensive career, Libbert has had the opportunity to photograph a plethora of leading figures in politics and the arts. Notable subjects include Alfred Hitchcock, Mariah Carey, Winston Churchill, Helen Mirren, Harold Pinter and Francis Bacon. His first solo exhibition was fittingly shown at the National Portrait Gallery, London, in 2012. Other galleries that have exhibited his work include the Stables Gallery within the Taos Center for the Arts, New Mexico, and the Whitechapel Gallery, London.

1 Information from the interview conducted by Jessica Feather on 3 April 2016.
2 Bridgeman Images, 'Neil Libbert: Chronicler of our Times', http://www.bridgemanimages.com/en-US/explore/news/new-collections/2014/June/neil-libbert
3 Information from the interview conducted by Jessica Feather on 3 April 2016.
4 Bridgeman Images, 'Neil Libbert: Chronicler of our Times', http://www.bridgemanimages.com/en-US/explore/news/new-collections/2014/June/neil-libbert
5 Information from the interview conducted by Jessica Feather on 3 April 2016.

Short History and Mission Statement

Ben Uri, 'The Art Museum for Everyone,' focuses distinctively on Art, Identity and Migration across all migrant communities to London since the turn of the twentieth century. It engages the broadest possible audience through its exhibitions and learning programmes. The museum was founded on 1 July 1915 by the Russian émigré artist Lazar Berson at Gradel's Restaurant, Whitechapel, in London's East End.

The name, 'The Jewish National Decorative Art Association (London), "Ben Ouri"', echoed that of legendary biblical craftsman Bezalel Ben Uri, the creator of the tabernacle in the Temple of Jerusalem. It also reflects a kinship with the ideals of the famous Bezalel School of Arts and Crafts founded in Jerusalem nine years earlier in 1906.

Ben Uri's philosophy is based on our conviction that fostering easy access to art and creativity at every level can add weight to our two guiding principles: 'The Dignity of Difference' and 'The Equality of Citizenship'. Ben Uri connects with over 300,000 people a year via its various creative platforms.

The museum positively and imaginatively demonstrates its value as a robust and unique bridge between the cultural, religious, political differences and beliefs of fellow British citizens.

Our positioning of migrant artists from different communities in London within the artistic and historical, rather than religious or ethnic, context of the British national heritage is both key and distinctive. Through the generous support of our 'Preferred Partner' Manya Igel Fine Arts, we provide free entry to all our exhibitions, removing all barriers to entry and participation.

Ben Uri offers the widest access to all its extensive programming and physical and virtual resources including exhibitions, publications, website and outreach through:

- The permanent collection: comprising 1300 works, the collection is dominated by the work of first- and second-generation émigré artists and is supported by a growing group of emerging contemporary artists who will be a principal attraction in the generations to come. The largest collection of its kind in the world, it can be accessed physically via continued exhibition, research, conservation and acquisitions, or virtually.
- Temporary exhibitions: curating, touring and hosting important internationally focused exhibitions of the widest artistic appeal which, without the museum's focus, would not be seen in the UK or abroad.
- Publications: commissioning new academic research on artists and their historical context to enhance the museum's exhibitions and visitor experience.
- Library and archive: a resource dating from the turn of the twentieth century, documenting and tracing in parallel the artistic and social development of both Ben Uri and Jewish artists, who were working or exhibiting in Britain, as part of the evolving British historical landscape.

- Education and community learning: for adults and students through symposia, lectures, curatorial tours and publications.
- Schools: Ben Uri's nationally available 'Art in the Open' programme via the 'National Education Network' and 'The London Grid for Learning' is available on demand to 16,000 schools across the United Kingdom. Focus-related visits, after-school art clubs, family art days and competitions are also regular features.
- Artists: regular artists' peer group programmes, international competitions, guidance and affiliation benefits.
- Wellbeing: a pioneering set of initiatives addressing the young with special needs and the elderly who may be living in some isolation or with early stages of dementia. The programmes recognise the significant importance of the carer within the relationship and uses art practice as an effective bridge for positive engagement.
- Website: provides an online educational and access tool, to function as a virtual gallery and reference resource for students, scholars and collectors.

The strength of the museum's growing collection and our active engagement with our public – both nationally and internationally – reinforces the need for Ben Uri to have a permanent museum and gallery in the heart of central London alongside this country's great national institutions. Only then will the museum be able to fulfil its potential and impact on the largest audiences from the widest communities from home and abroad.

We see our future as pioneering a new form of visitor engagement in the museum sector.

We will share our space with other émigré communities who will tell their own stories of journeys and life in London in modern times, and show their artists within a regular changing presentation. This new platform for emerging communities and artists will sit alongside, and as a key part of, the traditional museum matrix of collection, archive, exhibition, scholarship, learning and wellbeing designed to allow many different voices to attract, engage and stimulate large and diverse audiences from near and far.

Advisory Board and Patrons

Advisory Board

United Kingdom
Prof. Brian Allen, Hazlitt Group
Dr. Shulamith Behr, Courtauld
Dr. Richard Cork, Art Historian
Gill Hedley, Curator
Norman Lebrecht, Writer
Prof. Griselda Pollock, Scholar
Dr. Andrew Renton, Gallerist
Sir Norman Rosenthal, Curator
Sir Nicholas Serota
Dr. Evelyn Silber, Historian
Peyton Skipworth, Writer

Israel
Prof. Ziva Amishai-Maisels, Scholar
Shlomit Steinberg, Curator

Europe
Joel Cahan, Director
Dr. Eckhart Gillen, Curator
Dr. Leo Pávlat, Director
Dr. Danielle Spera, Director
Edward van Voolen, Curator

USA and Canada
Prof. Bruce Boucher, Director
Tom L Freudenheim, Writer
Derek Gillman, Auctioneer
Prof. Sander Gilman, Scholar
Susan T Goodman, Curator
Daniel Libeskind, Architect
Prof. Jack Lohman, Director

Patrons

Angela Abdoo
Clare Amsel
Gretha Arwas
Pauline and Daniel Auerbach
Esther and Simon Bentley
Miriam and Richard Borchard
Brandler Galleries, Brentwood
Jayne Cohen and Howard Spiegler
Marion and David Cohen
Sheila & Dennis Cohen Charitable Trust
Nikki and Mel Corin
Lynette and Robert Craig
Suzanne and Henry Davis
Rachel and Mike Dickson
Peter Dineley
Sir Harry and Lady Djanogly
Marion and Manfred Durst
The Fidelio Charitable Trust
Wendy Fisher
The Foyle Foundation
Franklin Family
Patsy and David Franks
Caroline Friedman

M & G M Frydman Foundation
Barbara and David Glass
David Glasser
Sue Glasser
Lindy and Geoffrey Goldkorn
Goldmark Gallery, Rutland
Madelaine and Craig Gottlieb
Eva Greenspan
Averil and Irving Grose
Gillian and Jeffrey Gruder QC
Tresnia and Gideon Harbour
Mym and Lawrence Harding
Peter Held
Sir Michael and Lady Heller
Joan Hurst
Manya Igel Fine Arts
Sandra and John Joseph
Annely Juda Fine Art
Neil Kitchener QC
Laura and Lewis Kruger
Hannah and David Latchman
Agnes and Edward Lee
Amanda and Howard Lewis
Jonathan and Veronique Lewis
Jacob Mendelson Scholarship Trust
Jewish Memorial Council
Lady Hannah and Lord Parry Mitchell
Robin and Edward Milstein
Montgomery Gallery, San Francisco
Hanno D Mott
Diana and Allan Morgenthau
Olesia and Leonid Nevzlin
Susan and Leo Noe
Opera Gallery, London
Osborne Samuel Gallery, London
Susan and Martin Paisner
Louis Perlman
Suzanne Perlman
Ingrid and Mike Posen
Simon Posen
Tis Prager
Janis and Barry Prince
Reed Smith LLP
Ashley Rogoff
Anthony and Lizzie Rosenfelder
Blick Rothenberg
Shoresh Charitable Trust
Rowena Fowler and Bernard Silverman
Dr. Michael Spiro
Lélia Pissarro and David Stern
Ann Susman
Jonathan Symons
Esther and Romie Tager
Myra Waiman
Judit and George Weisz
Eva and David Wertheim
Cathy Wills
The Maurice Wohl Charitable Foundation
Sylvie and Saul Woodrow
Matt Yeoman

Contributors

Katy Barron is an independent curator, writer and advisor, specializing in photography. She has curated photography exhibitions for museums and festivals in the UK and abroad and mentors a number of emerging photographers. Katy also advises photography collectors and attends portfolio reviews. Previously she worked at Purdy Hicks Gallery looking after their photographers.

Michael Berkowitz, a native of Rochester, NY, worked in the film emulsion melting department of the Eastman Kodak Company in the late 1970s. Professor of modern Jewish history at University College London, he is editor of *Jewish Historical Studies: Transactions of the Jewish Historical Society of England* (UCL Press). Most recently author of *Jews and Photography in Britain* (University of Texas Press, 2015), his research in photography has been supported by the Remarque Institute (NYU), Yad Vashem (Jerusalem), the United States Holocaust Memorial Museum (Washington, DC), the Center for Creative Photography (Tucson, AZ), the Ransom Center (Austin, TX), the University of London, and the British Society for the History of Science.

Zelda Cheatle is an independent curator who works nationally and internationally. She spent the 1980s at the Photographers' Gallery and opened her eponymous gallery in 1989. After 16 years of publishing and exhibiting contemporary photography led to her collecting for a fund, and exhibiting the collection. Curating, teaching at various universities, some writing, some consulting on collections, and enjoyable portfolio reviewing are all part of Zelda Cheatle's daily life.

Jessica Feather is currently Allen Fellow at the Paul Mellon Centre for Studies in British Art, and was previously Curator of Works on Paper at the Walker Art Gallery, Liverpool.

Saskia Rubin holds a Masters in History of Art from the Courtauld Institute of Art, and is the Curatorial Assistant for this exhibition.

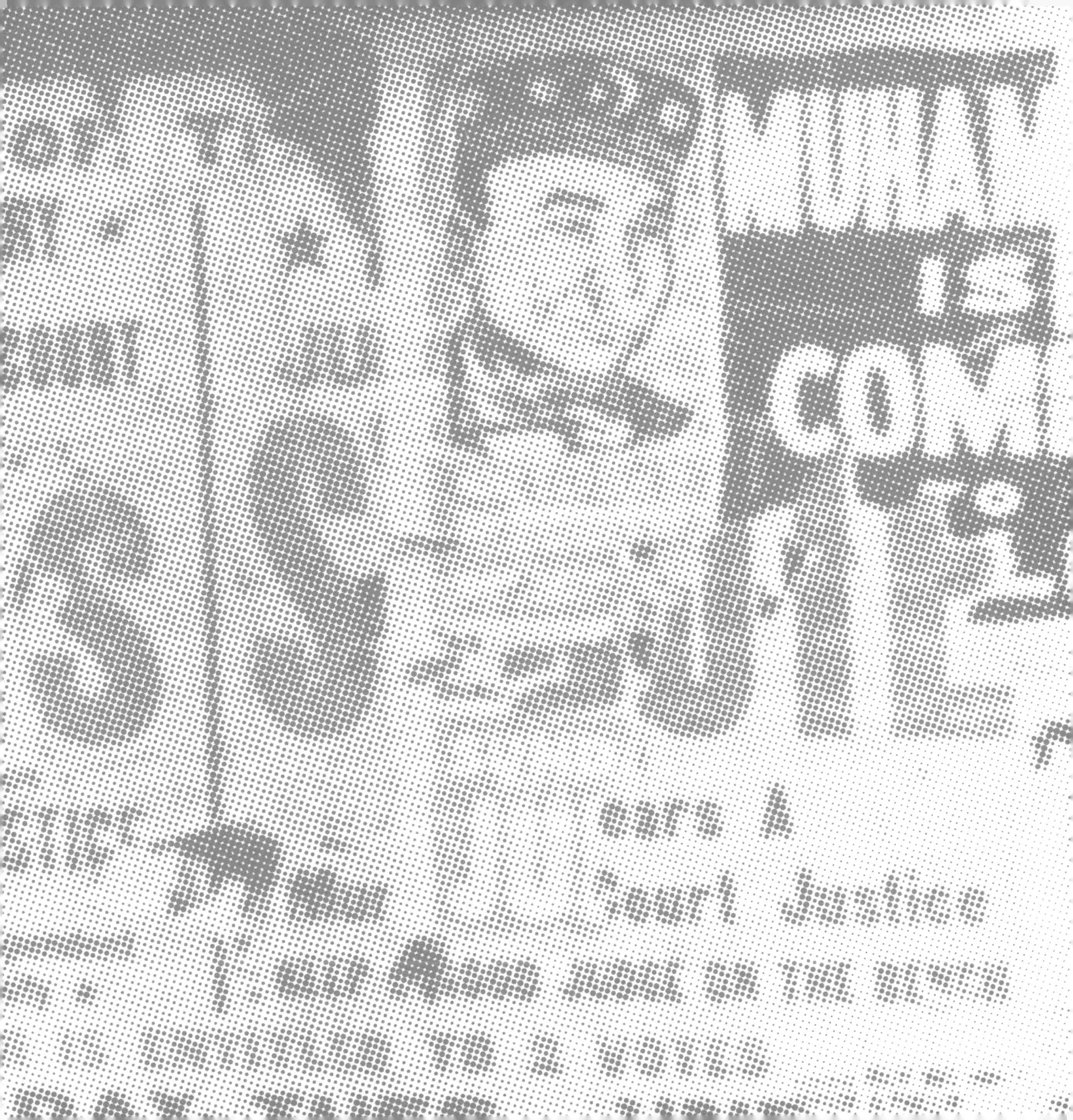

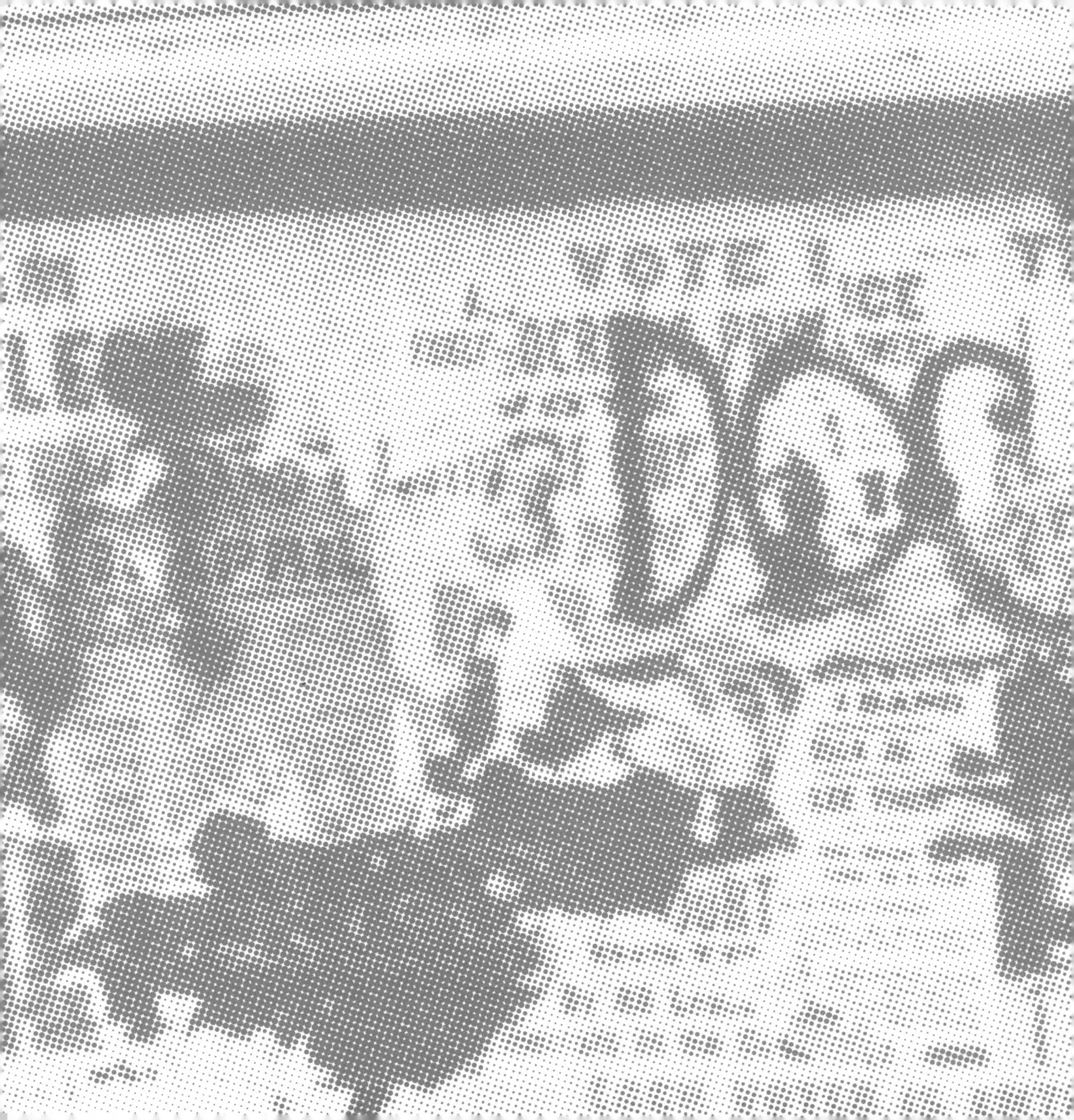